T0147162

Endorsements

"James Loftin lifts the curtain on how we can live with clarity and intentionality, unleashing the potential of a life that is aligned with God's purposes. This is a treasure trove of biblical insight from an experienced guide." —Steve Richardson, president, Pioneers USA, Orlando, FL

"A must-read. It is creative in its design and expression, using a familiar designation of who we are in such a fresh way that you want to read the next page." —Maxie Dunnam, author, pastor, and president emeritus of Asbury Theological Seminary, Memphis, TN

"A refreshing call to leave the world of small dreams and embark on a lifetime journey of maximum impact for God's glory. With a pastor's heart, a scholar's keen insight, and the apostolic zeal of one who has spent decades in global ministry, Loftin spells out in practical terms how to be intentional in reclaiming and maintaining our identity as the light of the world." —Brent Fulton, founder/catalyst, ChinaSource, Sacramento, CA

"The perfect mix of inspiration, practical application, and biblical wisdom. His call to shine stirs my heart to connect to what God is doing in the most strategic way possible!" —Emily Osburne, marketing director, Generous Giving, Orlando, FL

"This is a timely reminder that the light of Christ is within us and a guide for the ongoing spiritual renewal needed to shine in the darkness." —Kevin Wolley, captain B-767 (retired), FedEx Express, Portland, OR

"The world needs Christians who are strategic and gracious about living out their faith in ways that change lives and communities. This book leads us there." —Stacia Glavas, founder/CEO, New Life Mission, Melbourne, FL

"This book challenges, emboldens, and provides practical steps for ordinary Jesus followers who hunger to move beyond a consumer faith and maximize their unique impact in the world." —Chris Goff, pastor, the Hub Church, Thomasville, GA

"The call to *be the light of the world* has always felt like an unattainable cliché. This is the first book I've read that is deep, practical, and effective in helping readers understand the deeper meaning of shining as we follow Jesus." —Pete Marra, vice president of innovation, the Colson Center, Lexington, KY

"James Loftin forgot more about missions than I will ever know, but he communicates in a practical way for the busy pastor, the overwhelmed missions leader, and others who want to shine but are frustrated." —Win Greene, author and pastor, Trinity United Methodist Church, New Kingstown, PA

"Using Bible study and real-life stories, this book shows us what we can do and what God expects us to do as the light of the world. It is an inspiration for change, and perfect for small group study. I recommend it wholeheartedly!" —C. Ray Hayes, senior director, Hunter Lewis LLC, and chancellor emeritus of the University of Alabama System, Tuscaloosa, AL

"*Born to Shine* delivers inspiration as well as practical ways to live out the mission of Jesus. If there was ever a time for light to shine out in darkness, it is now." —Tom Cochran, national director of church engagement, Destiny Rescue USA, Palm Bay, FL

"James Loftin reflects on mission not simply as an idea that Christians warmly affirm, but as a practice that requires close attention to how we can be more consistent, strategic, and less selfish ... a helpful resource for individuals, classes, and groups who seek to refine the missional fires of their faith." —David F. White, author and professor of Christian education, Austin Presbyterian Theological Seminary, Austin, TX

"*Born to Shine* reminds us that the light within us is not to merely brighten the places where we live. Our shining can reach the faraway dark corners of the world." —John Johnson, founder and president of His Instruments of Worship, Memphis, TN

"*Born to Shine* is a pragmatic and insightful book from a passionate, dedicated, and respectful leader. It helped me revisit my path and refine my future direction." —Allen Mu, missionary with FMCD, Germany

"Practical, convicting, eye opening, biblically grounded, authentic, and necessary for today's Christian." —Christie Smith, family life local guide with CRU, Tuscaloosa, AL

"*Born to Shine* is a blueprint to maximize your impact for the Kingdom and help you see your mission from a totally different perspective." —Patrick Snipes, senior vice president-trading, FHN Financial, Memphis TN

"Filled with timely and provocative illustrations and challenging calls to discipleship, you will be glad you or your small group invested the time to explore and respond to the light ideas offered here." —Billy Still, author and United Methodist minister (retired), Brighton, CO

"A call to Spirit-filled discipleship which is intentional, strategic, and cross-cultural. There is not a more timely message for the church at this hour." —John Tanksley, orthopedic surgeon, Hutchinson, KS

"A fresh, insightful, relevant, and important book for all who are longing to shine the light of God into darkness. This book will shed light on the path of your life and ministry." —Asia Williamson, leadership development catalyst, Lausanne Movement, London, United Kingdom

"I loved the lines 'Right now, the Spirit is pursuing the abused, the hurting, and those who have never heard the good news. It is God's nature and mission to chase away darkness with truth, mercy, and grace.' *Born to Shine* is helping me face the realities of light and darkness." —Josh Womack, founder and CEO, Womack Financial, Dallas, TX

"A useful, thought-provoking primer for Christians wanting to live out their faith in ways that illuminate God's grace as demonstrated in the gift of Jesus." —Randall D. Noel, attorney, Memphis, TN

BORN TO SHINE

Reclaiming Your Identity as the Light of the World

JAMES LOFTIN

WESTBOW
PRESS®
A DIVISION OF THOMAS NELSON
& ZONDERVAN

WestBow Press books may be ordered through booksellers or by contacting:

WestBow Press
A Division of Thomas Nelson & Zondervan
1663 Liberty Drive
Bloomington, IN 47403
www.westbowpress.com
844-714-3454

Because of the dynamic nature of the Internet, any web addresses or links contained in this book may have changed since publication and may no longer be valid. The views expressed in this work are solely those of the author and do not necessarily reflect the views of the publisher, and the publisher hereby disclaims any responsibility for them.

The cover art and concept as well as the interior graphics and illustrations were provided by Craig Thompson and Disciple Design in Memphis, Tennessee.

ISBN: 978-1-6642-8044-1 (sc)
ISBN: 978-1-6642-8045-8 (hc)
ISBN: 978-1-6642-8043-4 (e)

Library of Congress Control Number: 2022918780

Print information available on the last page.

WestBow Press rev. date: 11/16/2022

To all those who push forward
in the face of countless obstacles
to announce and exhibit
the unconditional, transforming grace of Jesus Christ
in new ways and in unreached areas.
The world is a better place and God is glorified
because of the sacrificial lives of witnesses like
the Apostle Paul, Hudson Taylor, William Wilberforce,
Amy Carmichael, Moses Xie, Martin Luther King Jr.,
and
Pauline Hord.

Contents

Preface

God created you with a purpose and capacity to impact the world more than you imagine. Empowered by the Holy Spirit, your words and actions can shine near and far in such a way that lost and hurting people will be transformed by the grace of Jesus Christ. Using the biblical theme of light, *Born to Shine* provides more than inspiration and examples of faithful living. It presents practical guidance on how Christ followers can shine more brightly for the good of the world and for God's glory. You are the light of the world. God invites you to reclaim that identity with intentionality, urgency, and excellence.

This book is based on my understanding of an overarching biblical theme and decades of interaction with Christ followers around world who are trying to faithfully share and demonstrate the good news. I don't pretend that there is an original thought in this book, but this mix of theology and compassion is "classic James Loftin," as one old friend noted. I am thankful for the encouragement and challenge I've received from the witness of pioneers like John Wesley, Hudson Taylor, Gladys Aylward, William Carey, William Booth, Elisabeth Elliot, Moses Xie, William Wilberforce, Frederick Douglass, and Martin Luther King Jr. I have also been blessed by the contributions of thought leaders like David J. Bosch, John Piper, David Platt, Alan Hirsch, Carl Medearis, Timothy Tennent, Maxie Dunnam, Francis Chan, Nicky Gumbel, and others who are creatively addressing our role in the mission of God. With a heart full of gratitude to God and these witnesses, I want to do all I can to address darkness and invite people to experience the light of Jesus Christ. This book is part of my response to God's invitation to shine.

Language Choices

I use the words "missions," "mission," and "outreach" interchangeably. All refer to our partnership with God to proclaim the good news of Jesus's life, death, and resurrection and demonstrate God's grace through acts of compassion.

When I do not capitalize the word "*church*," I am referring to a local church or community. When I capitalize the word "Church," I am referring to the entire Christian Church. Regardless of geography, denomination, age, gender, ethnicity, education, ordination, nationality, or ability, all God's children are part of the Church.

Be the Change

At the end of each chapter, I have included a section titled "Be the Change." This is an opportunity to stop reading and begin considering what the content implies about your life and future. If you're reading the book with others, there are suggestions for interaction. Most importantly, there is guidance for talking with God and taking practical steps to shine more brightly. If you take time to think through these questions and jot down some notes, you will enjoy the reading more and you will open yourself more fully to the invitation God is making to you. Day by day, you will reclaim your identity as the light of the world.

I pray that God uses *Born to Shine* to encourage and equip you to shine brighter and higher than you ever imagined. To God be the glory!

Acknowledgments

I am indebted to many kind souls, but I must begin with the Source of every good and perfect gift. Without the forgiveness of God, the Spirit's guiding and empowering presence in my life, and the certainty that light overcomes darkness, I could not take my next breath, much less write a book. All those included in the incomplete list below are gifts from God.

I thank God for Sam Morris. God used him to get me started on my journey of faith in Jesus. Sam showed our gang of teenagers in 1970 that God is real and Jesus is close. He believed in us and encouraged us to believe that God would use us to change the world. The most important aspects of my approach to ministry are directly related to Sam's influence: reading God's Word, praying with others, and sharing Jesus's love. Without this foundation, I would have had little desire or confidence to lift high the light of Christ.

Special thanks go to my band of brothers: Tommy Artmann, David White, and Billy Still. Their love and encouragement over six decades, and especially the past six years, have kept me honest, relatively sane, and optimistic about God's ongoing work in our lives. Our weekly discussions continue to help me sharpen my understanding of grace, my appreciation of beauty, and my focus on the urgency of living fully each day. Each brother made valuable contributions to this manuscript.

A warm embrace of gratitude also goes to Maxie Dunnam. As a "world Christian," he understands life and faith with a gracious global perspective. Maxie hired me twice because he saw things I could not see. His confidence in me and constant love continue to propel me to enthusiastically engage in God's mission with my feet, voice, and pen.

This book would not have happened without the support of FollowOne International, the nonprofit ministry I launched in 2004 and continue to lead. I thank God for our wise, kind, and Christ-focused board of directors: Todd Massey, Tom Long, Soup Campbell, Tom Pittman, and Pete Marra. I am also grateful for the FollowOne supporters and the hundreds of friends who have participated in our short-term trips to Asia. Laura Messina has served with me at FollowOne for seventeen years. Her sharp mind, honest but gracious communication style, courage, and love for Jesus have pulled me into deeper waters of faith and witness.

I am grateful for a long list of churches, including Christ Church in Memphis, Tennessee, First United Methodist in Thomasville, Georgia, Crossroad Church in Jacksonville, Florida, and Northwest Bible Church in Dallas, Texas. As I coached the leaders of these and other churches, their questions and insights helped me better understand the potential and challenges of congregations who wish to shine with excellence.

Emily Osburne fielded my first queries about the possibility of writing a book in 2014. Her coaching and encouragement helped me focus and eventually believe that I could publish a book. Warm thanks to Emily, Carah Lynn Billups, Chris Goff, Carey Phillips, Bob Easley, Win Green, Mindy Eichorn, and others who reviewed early drafts and made suggestions.

I am thankful Craig Thompson and Disciple Design in Memphis, Tennessee. The art and visual tools they created for the book help us grasp and remember important truths. I also appreciate the staff of WestBow Press, a division of Thomas Nelson and Zondervan. Their encouraging and professional assistance moved *Born to Shine* from a concept in my computer to the reality of print.

Lastly, I offer great thanks to my family circle, people who are family by blood and by grace. In a variety of ways these good folks supported me during this writing project. In addition to those mentioned earlier, I offer a hug of appreciation to Runner, Kerry, Rob, Kathy, Ray, Pat, Richard, Layton, Russell, Meme, Joanne, Todd, Emily, Tom, Rhonda, Dave, Jonathan, Jose, Richard, Melissa, Kevin, Jane, Brent, David, Penny, Beverly, John, Ashely, Paul, Jane, Carolyn, Jeff, and Heather.

Other than Jesus, no one provided more support and inspiration for this project than my wife, Vivien. She is strong but gentle and has faith not unlike that of Sarah, Esther, Ruth, Naomi, Deborah, and Mary Magdalene. Thank you for shining so brightly and believing that God can use anyone, including your husband.

Introduction

So God created human beings in his own image. In the image of
God he created them; male and female he created them.

—Genesis 1:27 NLT

I was born at Baptist Hospital in Jackson, Mississippi. A host of doctors, nurses, and technicians were there to assist my mom. My family's pastor came to the hospital and prayed for us. My wife was born at her two-room home in Shenyang, China. A midwife was there to assist her mom. They didn't have a pastor, a church, or any knowledge of Jesus. Regardless of where, when, and how we begin life, all children have great potential. God creates us with the capacity to communicate, learn, love, laugh, believe, and much more. In his classic book on running, Christopher McDougall asserts that humans have the innate capacity to run distances far longer than most of us attempt or imagine.[1] In Matthew 5:14, Jesus looked his disciples in the eyes and made a much more shocking declaration: "You are the light of the world." He is looking into your eyes now and making that same statement.

We are created in the image of God. One aspect of God's image is our Creator's gracious willingness to bring light into darkness. When Jesus identified his first and all other disciples as the light of the world, he announced that in the core of our redeemed souls is the ability and passion to spread the light of Christ. This is our spiritual DNA. You were made for more than the enjoyment of your forgiveness and the other blessings of God. You were made to shine. Borrowing a phrase from Watchman Nee, shining is part of the "normal Christian life."[2]

Fully Alive

As we allow God's Spirit to shine through our words and actions, we bring God glory, and we join God's mission to transform the world with the love of Jesus. This intentional shining actualizes an important aspect of who we are as God's children. It is easy to see real but lesser examples of actualization all around us.

My ninety-pound yellow Lab named Sully was a faithful friend. I loved him, and in his canine way, Sully loved me. I enjoyed letting Sully go outside first thing each morning. As I moved toward the door, his tail wagged wildly, and he bounced up and down in anticipation. Once released, my four-legged "son" tore off in a dead run, searching for any squirrel, armadillo, rabbit, or bird that had dared to invade his turf. I was always amazed at his speed, the sound of his pounding feet, and what appeared to be a smile on his face. In those moments, Sully was simply being a dog. He was not created to lie on a bed in an air-conditioned home. His DNA gave him the desire and ability to find and retrieve. He was born to run, and he had not forgotten this key element of his identity. When he ran around using his great gifts of speed, sight, and smell, Sully was fully alive!

Thomas Merton (1915–1968) wrote about this same attribute of creation. "A tree gives glory to God by being a tree. For in being what God means it to be, it is obeying [God]. It 'consents,' so to speak, to [God's] creative love."[3] Rather than consenting to God's purposes for us, we humans often forget what we are created to be and do. Just as we forget to exercise our physical bodies, we forget to exercise our spiritual muscles. We easily and often wander away from our core identity as the light of the world. We allow distractions, called "baskets" in Matthew 5:15, to limit our shining. But when we consciously accept, celebrate, and actualize this identity, we are truly alive, and we shine God's light with boldness and grace.

Shining Now

Planet earth has perhaps never needed light, love, and grace more than it does today. Darkness often seems to be winning. In addition to the darkness caused by natural disasters like pandemics, fires, and deadly storms, profound suffering is produced by our selfish and sinful tendencies rooted in the failure of Adam and Eve. I can hardly bear to watch or read the news. But there is hope. Jesus is alive and well, and there are over two billion Christ followers on our beautiful but broken planet. God is using the Church to bring light to darkness.

Sadly, the response of the Church—you and me—to God's invitation is less than complete or excellent. The Church has much to celebrate about our work in the world, but statistics reveal that we are making little progress in addressing the needs of lost and hurting people.[4] Millions of souls are untouched by the light of the Church. Our shining is having less impact than it could. Many of us don't have a plan to shine. We just hope. We are not intentional. Our responses are often reactionary and haphazard, and far below the excellence that gracious God deserves. We can do better, but that involves a change in our attitude and approach. And that change needs to happen as soon as possible. The unmet needs of those in darkness are urgent.

Since you chose to read a book like this, I'm certain that you are already aware of the encroaching darkness, and you are addressing needs in your family, your community, and the world. This is not a *should* book or a call to *do more*. It's an invitation to shine *smarter*. Perhaps you feel overwhelmed by the countless needs that scream for your attention. Perhaps you don't feel that you are shining effectively or consistently. I understand. Please read my words as an invitation from one less-than-perfect Christ follower to another, as "one beggar showing another where to find bread."[5] Whatever is going on in your life, God has given you the desire and ability to be the light of the world. This book invites you to celebrate how you are shining today, and then take steps to lift your lantern higher.

The Invitation

Born to Shine is about God's love, our response to that infinite love, and the hope that flows from love. The older I get, the more I grasp God's unconditional love for all of creation, including me. The love of God shines in a way that grabs my soul and causes me to worship, laugh, cry, and work to lift up the lamp of God's grace. I pray that you will join me in this journey to more fully accept God's love and God's invitation to shine. As you grasp the gracious hand of God, the Spirit will fan the flame of your life so high that you will begin to believe that Jesus knows what he is talking about. You are indeed the light of the world.

This journey to shine more brightly will be driven by joy as well as gratitude and urgency. Eric Liddell (1902–1945) was a Scottish missionary to China and an Olympic runner. In the 1981 Oscar-winning film *Chariots of Fire*, Ian Chesterton, playing Liddell, speaks of his desire and ability to run fast: "When I run, I feel God's pleasure."[6] I pray that God uses the words of this book to provide joy, confidence, and practical guidance as you run with Jesus in his urgent mission. May the Spirit help you reclaim your identity as the light of the world, and may your shining bring a smile to the face of Jesus and healing light to the world. More than you have imagined, your life can communicate grace and bring solutions that change the world for God's glory.

Section I
LIGHT

CHAPTER 1

This Little Light of Mine

You are the light of the world. A town built on a hill cannot be hidden. Neither do people light a lamp and put it under a bowl. Instead they put it on its stand, and it gives light to everyone in the house. In the same way, let your light shine before others, that they may see your good deeds and glorify your Father in heaven.

—Matthew 5:14–16

Highlights

> Jesus calls us to lift our lanterns high by living in such a way that our lives have maximum impact on the world.
> To shine more brightly, most of us will need a transformation of our attitude as well as our actions.
> When our life priorities line up with God's mission to redeem and bless the world, we reclaim our identity as the light of the world and amazing things happen.

Like most children in my neighborhood, each summer I participated in a children's program that was called vacation Bible school. For one week, church volunteers entertained and encouraged us with games, Bible stories, snacks, and fun music. We sang many songs, but I particularly remember "This Little Light of Mine." We sang verses like, "Hide it under a bushel? No," and "Spread it all over my hometown? Yes." My understanding of the song's message was that I should be kind and say a good word for Jesus when I get a chance.

For too long, I overlooked the deeper meaning of "This Little Light of Mine" as well as Jesus's words in Matthew 5:14–16. Perhaps you have also. In this opening section of the Sermon on the Mount, Jesus makes at least two bold statements. First, as followers of Jesus, we are the light of the world. This is the *what* of the message. I can hear one of his first-century listeners replying, "But, Lord, I thought you are the Light of the world?" They would have been correct, but only partially so. As amazing as it sounds, God has decided to use people of faith in the holy mission to bring light to the darkness of the world. We can shine because the Spirit of God resides in us (Romans 8:9; 1 Corinthians 6:19–20; 12:13).

In the *what* of this passage, Jesus reminds his followers of who we are. We are those who once were blind but now see. We were in darkness, but now we walk in the light of life (Luke 19:10; John 8:12). The Apostle Peter said it this way: "But you are a chosen people, a royal priesthood, a holy nation, God's special possession, that you may declare the praises of him who called you out of darkness into his wonderful light" (1 Peter 2:9). As a response to God's light in your life, take a minute now to make this affirmation to God and to yourself. Say these words as loud as you dare: I am the light of the world. Say it again: I am the light of the world. If you are hesitant, ask God to help you believe what Jesus has declared to be true about you.

Jesus goes on to make a second bold statement as he addresses the *how* of being the light of the world. This is the part of Jesus's message that is easily underappreciated. "Neither do people light a lamp and put it under a bowl. Instead they put it on its stand, and it gives light to everyone in the house" (Matthew 5:15; Luke 8:16). A lantern lifted high will have much greater impact on darkness than an equally nice lantern placed close to the floor or under a bowl. Jesus explicitly encourages us to lift our lamps high.

It's important to understand the terms used in this light passage in Matthew. Jesus is referring to items that were common in first-century homes. The main room often had a cooking area and containers (bowl, bushel, jar, or basket) used to store flour, grains, water, and oil. The home also had a source of light and a lampstand. What is usually translated as "light," "candle," or "lamp" refers to something that Jesus's listeners certainly had in their homes: a saucerlike lamp that may have been no more than a wick floating in oil.[7]

What is translated as "candlestick" or "lampstand" refers to anything used to lift the source of light as high as possible to provide maximum light in the room. A lampstand could have been a wooden pedestal or a shallow outcropping or shelf in a wall. More elaborate lampstands included a sliding shaft to raise and lower the lamp. Often in scripture, the words "lampstand" or "candlestick" refer to the seven-branched candlestick of the tabernacle or temple. This ornate and ceremonial lamp is not the type found in the Matthew 5 passage. Jesus is referring to a simple, inexpensive lamp and lampstand that were commonly used in homes.

These details of the passage are significant to the extent that they amplify the core message. Darkness is real. People need light. God is the source of light. We have the ability to shine. The degree to which we reflect God's light is significantly influenced by our own decisions, the way we choose to position and invest our light.

High Lights, High Cost

Shining in a way that only impacts a few people often takes little effort. Bolder shining can be costly. Throughout history, people have sometimes found themselves in dark situations that require sobering decisions at the crossroad of shining and suffering. Born into a devout Christian family in Forchtenberg, Germany, in 1931, Sophie Scholl developed a strong Christian faith that emphasized the dignity of every human being. Motivated by her faith, Sophie joined other teenagers in opposition to the Nazi ideology. She was executed by guillotine for distributing antiwar leaflets soon after joining the movement. Her last words were "How can we expect righteousness to prevail when there is hardly anyone willing to give himself up individually to a righteous cause. Such a fine, sunny day, and I have to go, but what does my death matter, if through us, thousands of people are awakened and stirred to action?"[8] Sophie faced a challenge that few of us will encounter, but notice the principle she followed. The decisions we make for God's righteous cause in our day-to-day existence impact the number of souls that are awakened and stirred by the grace of God.

John the Baptist was another bright witness. "He came as a witness to testify concerning that light, so that through him all might believe. He himself was not the light; he came only as a witness to the light. The true light that gives light to everyone was coming into the world" (John 1:7–9). This passage echoes the emphasis of Matthew 5:16. The paramount goal of being light is that others might glorify God—that is, to honor and worship the Lord of light. Our shining is all about God's greater glory. As the children of God, we pray that people who observe our words and deeds will respond like those who witnessed Jesus's healing of the possessed boy in Luke 9: "They were all amazed at the greatness of God" (verse 43; see also Luke 5:26).

Although our obedience, service, and love are important to God's light mission, we are not the source or power of light. We are like lampstands, mirrors, and moons. The size or composition of the lampstand is not important. Of quintessential importance is the light itself. Commenting on the biblical phrase "the light of the world," American theologian Albert Barnes (1798–1870) wrote, "It is preeminently applied to Jesus … because he is, in the moral world, what the sun is in the natural world. The apostles, Christian ministers, and all Christians, are lights of the world, because they, by their instructions and example, show what God requires, what is the condition of man, what is the way of duty, peace, and happiness, the way that leads to heaven."[9] Sophie, John the Baptist, and all Christians throughout history have been able to shine only because Jesus, the light of the world, abides in our lives by his Holy Spirit.

Attitudes and Action

One might assume that Jesus's meaning in Matthew 5 is that Christ followers *inevitably* shine in the same sense that a city on a hill can't be hidden. Some might believe that we *must* shine since the Spirit of God is within us. The text, however, describes a human-divine partnership. The presence of Jesus in our lives provides the light, but we determine how we will shine and reflect his light. Jesus calls us to lift our lanterns high as an act of cooperation in his enterprise of bringing light to darkness. Shining may be inevitable for the children of God, but our decisions influence how brightly we shine. And our decisions are influenced by our assumptions and attitudes.

Be honest about the attitudes you have regarding exercising, visiting a national park, filing your income tax return, buying the perfect birthday present for a loved one, reading a good book in a comfortable setting, going to the dentist, cleaning your bathroom, and going to lunch with an old friend. Some activities are dreaded, endured only as a necessity of life, and postponed as much as possible. Other activities are anticipated with joy and excitement. What about the activities that are directly related to your faith: reading your Bible, going to a worship service, making donations to your church, serving the homeless, and sharing the good news with someone experiencing darkness? If you are honest, you will admit that negative factors like shame, social pressure, fatigue, misinformation, and a lack of expectancy influence some aspects of your Christian life. In this opening chapter, I hope you will get in touch with your attitude toward being involved in God's mission.

To shine more brightly, most of us will need a transformation of our attitude as well as our actions. As you seek God's help in reclaiming your identity as the light of the world, the Spirit will change how you see your role in God's mission and the way you live out your faith. In this transformation, passion will replace dread, urgency will replace idleness, expectancy will replace a lack of faith, engagement will replace spectatorship, intentionality will replace haphazardness, confidence will replace insecurity, and daily shining will replace episodic shining. A casual approach to shining for God will be replaced by an attitude of adventure that seeks to change the world and present Jesus with an excellent gift.

Let us return to the central challenge of this chapter. Our Savior is calling us to live in such a way that our lives will have maximum impact on the world with the good news of God's love. We are invited to live as lights shining brightly in darkness. This high-light approach to life does not happen without focus and work. Think again about Jesus's lantern illustration. To get a lantern to the most strategic place in a room, we might have to string a rope from the ceiling or fashion a lampstand that can hold the lamp high. This strategic shining takes effort. There is a risk and a cost for anyone who determines to reflect the maximum amount of God's light. But the glory of God and the urgent needs of the world deserve our best.

Light from Chickens

Regardless of age, geography, education, or other factors, every child of God can bring light to darkness in ways that are wonderful and often shocking. Several years ago, I had the privilege of teaching a group of twenty-five pastors in rural Asia. These loving and courageous disciples were serving their churches and communities faithfully, but their hearts burned with a desire to influence more lives for Christ. For two weeks, we explored their question "How can we be more effective in mission?" Our times of worship, sharing, and prayer were powerful and unforgettable. I gained far more from them than I contributed.

Two years later, I had the opportunity to revisit some of my former students. After a generous meal, my hosts were anxious to show me something that required a long car ride. When we finally pulled up to a group of chicken coops, the pastors began laughing at the confused expression on my face. Here is my memory of how one brother interpreted the sight in front of me:

> You invited us to think creatively about how we could take the good news to places beyond our imagination. We are simple farmers with little education and few resources, but we started praying. The Lord answered our prayers. We received a vision that fits perfectly with who we are and where we live. God invited us to share his love in the neighboring country. The border is less than thirty kilometers from here. It has few Christians, and they have had a famine for many years. We continued

praying and thinking, and God gave us a plan. One of the traditional meals in that country is made with a special fowl that is now impossible to find there. We bought some of these birds in our country and began to raise them here. By God's grace, one of our brothers got permission from both governments to deliver and sell the birds across the border. Once a month, we take a truckload of the birds to that country. But we take more. A hidden compartment under the birds is filled with Bibles. It is our joy to share physical and spiritual food with our neighbors.

These farmers had an impact far beyond what their wealth, training, or sophistication would suggest. They had great faith and a bold attitude about shining. Jesus meets us where we are and takes us where he pleases. When our life priorities line up with God's mission to redeem and bless the world, we reclaim our identity as the light of the world and amazing things happen.

From Genesis to Revelation, we see that God is the creator and source of light. Jesus identified himself with words like "I am the Light of the world" (John 8:12), but he identified his followers with the same words. We will explore this more deeply in chapter five, but here is God's mysterious plan: God has chosen to use people of faith as the light of the world so that we may bring God's salvation to the ends of the earth (Isaiah 49:6). Regarding light and life, Jesus extends three invitations:

> Jesus calls us to worship him. Jesus invites us to walk into his arms of healing. This is the embrace of grace, conversion. The Light takes up residence in those who place their faith in Jesus.
> Jesus calls worshippers to follow in his steps. Jesus invites us to do what he does. This is the divine–human partnership. Those who love God shine by loving their neighbors as God loves us.
> Jesus calls followers to walk like he walks. Jesus was lifted up on Calvary once and for all as a beacon of grace. Those who

love God and our neighbors seek to lift our lanterns as high as possible for God's glory, regardless of the cost.

As you acknowledge the work of the Holy Spirit in your life, you will begin to believe that you really can impact the world. This awareness might even make you want to shout and sing. "This Little Light of Mine" is far more than a children's song. It is a song with an attitude of boldness and expectation. This chorus encouraged unity and steadied the nerves of civil rights workers in America in the 1960s, and it has fanned the flames of change in countless other settings. Today it continues to remind us of the truth that light will always overcome darkness. Even a small light can have great impact if it is placed strategically. Sing these words, and sing with an *attitude*:

> This little light of mine, I'm gonna let it shine
> This little light of mine, I'm gonna let it shine
> This little light of mine, I'm gonna let it shine
> Let it shine, let it shine, let it shine.[10]

May God give you a greater sense of confidence, adventure, courage, and unity with God's family as you march forward to bring light to the lost and hurting. You are the light of the world. Believe it. Sing it. Live it.

Be the Change

CHAPTER 1: THIS LITTLE LIGHT OF MINE

Consider

- ➤ What are your hopes and expectations as you begin reading *Born to Shine*?
- ➤ Consider why you are reading this book at this point in your life.

Interact

> ➤ Share about someone who has recently been the light of the world to you.
> ➤ What holds you back from fully believing that you are the light of the world?

Pray

> ➤ Thank God for those in your life who have pointed your attention to God's love by being the light of the world.
> ➤ Ask God to use this book to make you shine more brightly. Admit your fears about how shining more intentionally might change your life.
> ➤ Pray for Christians in East Asia as they work to share God's light with ethnic groups that have little or no understanding of God's goodness and presence.

Act

> ➤ Write a note of gratitude to someone who has recently shared God's light and love with you. Share something like "Thank you for letting God's light shine through you. You are the light of the world."
> ➤ Sing aloud "This Little Light of Mine" as you write the note of gratitude.

C H A P T E R 2

Haphazard Light

For you were once darkness, but now you are light in the Lord. Live as children of light.

—Ephesians 5:8

Highlights

- ➤ Many people talk about making a difference in the world, but Christians are uniquely called and equipped to be change agents.
- ➤ We can have some impact with random expressions of love in our daily lives, but when we take the effort to lift our lanterns high, God can use one life to impact thousands.
- ➤ The specific details of our lives influence how we shine, but they don't have to limit the impact of our shining.

"The Starfish Story" is part of a sixteen-page essay published by Loren Eiseley in 1969. Countless speakers have used this fable to inspire audiences around the world. Here is one version of the story. "A man was walking on the beach one day and noticed a boy who was reaching down, picking up a starfish and throwing it in the ocean. As he approached, he called out, 'Hello! What are you doing?' The boy looked up and said, 'I'm throwing starfish into the ocean'. 'Why are you throwing starfish into the ocean?' asked the man. 'The tide stranded them. If I don't throw them in the water before the sun comes up, they'll die' came the answer."[11]

At this point in the story, listeners are hooked. They see the dilemma. Starfish are in danger of dying on the shore, and a kind boy is trying to save them. What will the man say? Will the boy be devastated when he realizes that he cannot save them all? The story continues as the man responds to the boy. "'Surely you realize that there are miles of beach, and thousands of starfish. You'll never throw them all back, there are too many. You can't possibly make a difference.' The boy listened politely, then picked up another starfish. As he threw it back into the sea, he said, 'It made a difference for that one.'"[12] In response to this punch line, the listeners smile, begin nodding their heads, and some emit a moan of approval.

It is a nice story, but I emit a different kind of moan when I hear it now. It has never inspired me. While I affirm the boy's desire to make a difference, I reject the not-so-subtle message that the sentimental story communicates. It is sweetness without impact. Kindness without change. Benevolence without cost. The story encourages convenience over strategy. I see this story as another distraction from what God has called and empowered us to do. The starfish fable may encourage us to be kinder as we bump into needs, but it may also endorse a response to God's call that is far beneath our potential. It understates what God can do through one yielded life.

Remembering Jesus's message to his followers and the urgent needs of humankind, a better ending to the starfish story might go like this.

> "Young man, I see that you want to make a difference. God has given you this desire. This is exciting." As he speaks the man joins the boy in throwing back starfish after starfish. After several minutes of work, the man asks, "How many do you think we can save this way?" The boy thinks for a moment and replies, "If we work hard, I think we can save one hundred." Smiling, the wise man replies, "Would you like to save more? What would you say if I told you we could save a thousand or more?"

The boy's smile widens. "How can we save that many?" The man stops and looks at the lad. "I don't know the answer yet, but let's work on this. Let's find out why these starfish are washing up on shore. Maybe there is something we can do to help prevent so many from dying." The boy listens and adds, "Maybe people at the university can help." His mind keeps churning. "I bet my science class and scout troop will want to help also."

The two continue talking and throwing back starfish for hours. When they leave the beach, they do not forget the starfish. They do their homework and develop plans to impact more starfish than the boy ever imagined.

Make a Difference

People love to talk about making a difference in the world. Celebrities as diverse as Bill Gates, Bono, Dolly Parton, and Meghan Markle consistently demonstrate their passion to help people and improve the planet. Millions of socially conscious people organize and participate in efforts like *Make a Difference Day*, *Red Nose Day*, and countless local humanitarian projects. There is something within most of us that craves to be part of a movement that brings positive change to the world, our own communities, or even one other life. In addition to Jesus, many have written and spoken about this internal hunger.

> ➤ "Be who God meant you to be and you will set the world on fire." Catherine of Siena
> ➤ "The purpose of life is not to be happy. It is to be useful, to be honorable, to be compassionate, to have it make some difference that you have lived and lived well." Ralph Waldo Emerson
> ➤ "How wonderful it is that nobody need wait a single moment before starting to improve the world." Anne Frank
> ➤ "The purpose of life is to contribute in some way to making things better." Robert F. Kennedy

In January 2020, Spinditty posted a list of great songs that push for change. The list included the following:[13]

- "One Love," by Bob Marley and The Wailers, 1965
- "With My Own Two Hands," by Ben Harper, 2003
- "I Need to Wake Up," by Melissa Etheridge, 2005
- "If You're Out There," by John Legend, 2008
- "Make a Little Wave," by Demi Lovato and Joe Jonas, 2009
- "Change," by Carrie Underwood, 2009
- "Do Something," by Matthew West, 2012
- "One Man Can Change the World," by Big Sean, 2015

Just as "This Little Light of Mine" was used during the civil rights movement, music is almost always a part of social change. In an article for NPR, Anastasia Tsioulcas wrote, "Every revolution has its music."[14] In Lebanon, demonstrators rallied around "Baby Shark," taking the song far beyond the intent of the creators. "Do You Hear the People Sing?" from *Les Misérables* became a popular refrain at freedom protests in Hong Kong. Around the world, musicians, poets, prophets, and authors scream for better lives for those who are cheated, abused, forgotten, or dehumanized. Their words and music fan the flames of change.

The word "altruism" was used for the first time in the nineteenth century by Auguste Comte. He explains that altruism is related to "the elimination of the selfish desire and of egocentrism, as well as leading a life devoted to the well-being of others."[15] Some form of altruism has perhaps existed ever since humans lived in community. People of every faith and no faith at times demonstrate selfless kindness and altruism. But no person or group has more potential and should be more interested in altruism and making a difference than Christ followers. Jesus embodied altruism, and throughout history, Christ's followers have served and sacrificed in ways that cannot be explained by mere human kindness, Darwinism, psychology, or sociobiology.

As children of light (Ephesians 5:8), God calls us to shine. The Spirit within us gives us the desire and power to serve others and change the world in amazing ways. In the classic devotional *My Utmost for His Highest*, Oswald Chambers says it this way: "Remember what you are saved for—that the Son of God might be manifested in your mortal flesh."[16] When we receive the light of Christ by faith, the desire to share that light is a normal fruit of conversion. It is not specifically included in Paul's list of nine fruit of the Spirit (Galatians 5:22–23), but it is there. Through our love, joy, peace, patience, kindness, goodness, faithfulness, gentleness, and self-control, Christ followers shine. Although shining is a fruit of the Spirit, we have the power to short-circuit the intended system of light. In a candlelight worship service, ushers often light the candles only of the people seated on the ends of rows. Those people are expected to pass the light to their neighbors. A failure to share the light is as obtuse as it is unlikely, but it happens. Paul urged his coworkers to "not to receive God's grace in vain" (2 Corinthians 6:1). The Spirit within us compels us to shine, and if we listen closely, we will realize that the Spirit is also moving us to shine as brightly as possible.

The Importance of One

I dislike the story of a boy trying to save a few starfish because I understand that God's invitation to shine includes the goal of maximum impact. That goal may suggest large numbers of people, but it is appropriate to stop here and remember a basic truth: every life has eternal worth. Shining faithfully is not primarily about programs and statistics. It is about the value of each person. Perhaps that is the key point of the traditional starfish story. Our gracious heavenly Father loves the entire world. At the same time, the Lord focuses grace on each person as if he or she is the only soul in the universe.

It is easy, however, to overlook individuals on our path to shine on the masses. I once heard Tony Campolo describe his interchange with a man in front of a homeless ministry. The man looked and smelled as bad as the streets where he lived, but he was smiling as steam swirled above the cup in his hands. As Campolo attempted to negotiate past him on the sidewalk, their eyes met, and the man offered, "Do you want a drink of my coffee?" Campolo resisted an urge to jerk back in response to the germ-spreading invitation. By God's grace, he asked the man why he wanted to share his coffee. The happy man replied, "If the Lord has given me something this good, I ought to share it." Moved by the words, Campolo accepted the cup. "What can I give you in response," Campolo asked. The generous man threw up his arms as an invitation and said, "How about a hug!" Campolo hoped for a brief embrace, but it was a tight and long hug. The longer it lasted, the more Campolo relaxed. At that point, he recalled hearing Jesus's words, "Truly I tell you, whatever you did for one of the least of these brothers and sisters of mine, you did for me" (Matthew 25:40). Our desire to impact lives, change the world, and bring light to darkness is rooted in and empowered by God's indwelling presence in our lives. God's Spirit helps us see others, all others, with the eyes of Jesus. Every individual is valuable to God and worthy of our respect.

My vision is far less than perfect. I sometimes fail to see people the way Jesus sees me. Sometimes I do not recognize true greatness until it stands up in front of me. As dean of the chapel at Asbury Theological Seminary's campus in Orlando, I led weekly worship experiences for the community. At the beginning of each service, I routinely asked whether anyone had a guest. One day Professor Bill Patrick responded, "Yes. I'd like to introduce my friend Fred Rogers." It took a second before the name became clear in my brain: The *Fred Rogers*. *This is the sweater-wearing Christian minister and gracious shaper of young souls who is host of the television series* Mister Rogers' Neighborhood. *This is the guy that ends each episode by telling children, "You've made this day a special day, by just being you. There's no person in the whole world like you; and I like you just the way you are."*

As Rogers stood, I welcomed him and offered him an invitation: "Would you like to share anything?" He paused and then began: "Whenever I meet another person, I remind myself that this friend is a unique creation of God. I think of the space between us as holy ground and interact with her or him with that in mind." As I reimagine that encounter, I hear myself saying again what I whispered to myself that day: "Here is a great man, a man who sees people like Jesus sees us." Every person is created in the image of God and is valued by the Creator. When we remember that truth, we will treat each person with respect as we move forward to shine God's love on as many souls as possible.

It Was Convenient for Me

Although every person is important and every Christian can have far-reaching impact, our attitude about shining often does not line up with those truths. We tend to be random in our response to God's call to be the light of the world. I know about randomness. For the first two decades of my Christian journey, I tried to share God's light by what might be called "walking-around ministry." Wherever I walked or traveled, I tried to share and demonstrate God's love. I silently prayed for the people riding elevators with me. I bought meals for homeless folks I encountered. Those seated next to me on airplanes heard something from me about God's love. Families that moved onto my street were invited to church. Everywhere I went, I tried to be a good witness. It was nice approach to life, but my shining was totally haphazard. As I came across a starfish, I graciously pointed it to the ocean of God's love.

Amazingly, God blessed this approach to life and God's mission. Lives were impacted for Christ, but something was missing. My style of shining was predominantly a matter of personal convenience. I demonstrated and shared God's love wherever I went. I was not the light of the world as much as I was a light for those who were in my path every day. My potential impact was determined by my personal desires, responsibilities, and calendar. I didn't use these exact words, but my attitude and approach to shining could be illustrated by this prayer: "God, please use me today wherever I decide to go." The prayer of a person fully committed to being the light of the world is quite different: "God, please use me today wherever *you send me*."

If all our ancestors in the faith had followed this same lifestyle, I would probably not be writing as a Jesus follower today. I'm so thankful that courageous women and men decided to not be random in their witness. They decided to strategically move from one culture to another in the hope that they might shine brightly where no lantern had yet been lifted. People have gone out of their way to find me, serve me, and love me. Their actions were not haphazard or coincidental. They were intentional about sharing Jesus and shining God's love as brightly as possible.

We are all tempted to be random, even self-centered, in the way we participate in God's mission. We underestimate what might happen if we reclaim our identity as the light of the world and are intentional about shining for Jesus.

A One-Legged Scotsman

It is easy to see certain aspects of our lives as limitations on how we might make a difference in the world. George Scott (1835–1889) was a one-legged Scotsman who loved Jesus and wanted to shine brightly. Most people considered his physical state as a limiting factor, but the Scotsman believed he was called to be a missionary. When asked why he wanted to serve abroad, Scott replied, "I do not see those with two legs going, so I must." Upon arriving in China, Scott searched for a place where the love of Christ had not been proclaimed. God led him to Wenzhou, where he began a school that grew into a church planting movement. Wenzhou eventually became known as the "Jerusalem of China" because of the large number of Christians there. Some report that one of eight people there are now believers—a high percentage in a country that provides limited opportunities for public witness.[17] Many Wenzhou Christian businessmen have taken the gospel throughout China as well as to Europe and the Middle East. The light shared by a one-legged Scotsman has impacted millions.

Most of us have two legs, but we allow other realities of life to limit how we shine. The most common and restricting reality is our lack of intentionality. The specific details of our lives—such as our health, education, and finances—influence how we shine, but they don't have to limit the impact of our shining. Even the most gifted and successful people have limitations. Legendary singer-songwriter James Taylor once shockingly stated that he lacked proficiency in piano, guitar, and voice. He then shared the secret of his success: "My limitations are the containers the juice gets poured into."[18] God pours his Spirit into the container of your individual life, and those aspects that you perceive as limitations may be the very conduits Jesus uses to shine his love to others. As God's child, you are the light of the world. Your potential impact is huge—far beyond your wildest dreams.

Your lantern will have its own strategic place in God's work according to your gifts, limitations, calling, and other factors. You, not unlike George Scott, may want to fully live into the potential God has given you. You would rather offer long-term solutions to needs than temporary fixes. You would rather impact one thousand lives than one hundred lives. You want to shine brightly as the light of the world. Your desire to impact masses is evidence of the Holy Spirit's presence in your life, wooing you to shine in new ways for God's glory. Your attitude about the call to "live as children of light" (Ephesians 5:8) is changing, but you need more than inspiration. You need a plan that will connect your new attitude with effective action. Before jumping into action, take time to better understand the nature of light and darkness and reflect on the character and methodology of God.

Be the Change

CHAPTER 2: HAPHAZARD LIGHT

Consider

> ➤ Are there specific points in your history when you recall wishing, hoping, or praying, "I want to make a difference?"
> ➤ What circumstances drove you to utter that thought to yourself or God?
> ➤ How is that wish being fulfilled?

Interact

> ➤ Which person in this chapter best represents the way you shine? Explain.
>   o The boy throwing back starfish

- o   The man in the revised starfish story
- o   Tony Campolo
- o   The homeless man
- o   Mr. Rogers
- o   The author's haphazard approach to making a difference
- o   The one-legged missionary
- o   James Taylor
➤   Discuss the impact of adults as they respond to children who see needs and want to help.

Pray

➤   Talk with God about the things you do with focus and intentionality and some of the important things that you approach in a haphazard way.
➤   Pray for homeless people around the world and those who are trying to help them find homes and a future.

Act

➤   Write down one specific need in the world that concerns you today (illiteracy, disease, hunger, lack of access to the Bible, homelessness, and so on).
➤   List five things a person or group can do that would provide short-term relief to people with that need.
➤   What is one thing a person or group could do to address the long-term aspects of the need?

CHAPTER 3

Light and Life

And God said, "Let there be light," and there was light. God saw that the
light was good, and he separated the light from the darkness.

—Genesis 1:3–4

Highlights

> - The science of light is still not fully understood, but we know
>   that life is meaningless if not impossible without it.
> - The pain of darkness is universal, and millions continue to cry
>   out for the healing of light.
> - When we intentionally live in a way that helps people notice
>   the beauty of God, we are reclaiming our identity as the light
>   of the world.

God is the creator and the ongoing source of light. We are called to
be the light of the world, but answer this question: What is light? I
have not read science books since my freshman year in college, but to
adequately address the theme of this book, I felt compelled to dig into
the science of light. An appreciation of the nature of light will help us
more adequately grasp the meaning of Jesus's declaration that we are
the light of the world. I plead with all scientists to be gracious as you

read my lay summarization of very complicated scientific facts and theories.

You are able to read this book only because of the millions of photons produced by light sources and reflected off objects around you. Light is a key tool for perceiving the world around us, but it is much more. Light from the sun warms Earth, creates weather, and initiates the life-sustaining process called photosynthesis. Like many queries in life, it is far easier to ask the question "What is light?" than it is to get a straight answer.

The *Merriam-Webster Dictionary* offers over a dozen possible uses of this word, but the first definition is the most overarching. Light is "something that makes vision possible, the sensation aroused by stimulation of the visual receptors."[19] Another describes light as "a collection of one or more photons propagating through space as electromagnetic waves."[20] Another source offers: "Visible light is not inherently different from the other parts of the electromagnetic spectrum with the exception that the human eye can detect visible waves."[21] A thorough study of light forces a student to consider rays, reflection, refraction, electromagnetism, gamma radiation, radio waves, spectra, radiation, particles, waves, quantum theory, photons, bioluminescence, incandescence, lasers, color, and absorption. I was surprised to learn, however, that there is not yet a comprehensive and exhaustive explanation of light that has unanimous agreement among scientists.

A search for an explanation of light began when the first humans considered the differences between day and night. Thinkers like Pythagoras (c. 500 BC) are credited with voicing the earliest theories. Physicists preferred to think of light as either a wave or particle until Albert Einstein wrote about wave-particle duality and special relativity. Since the mid–twentieth century, some physicists have considered a theory known as quantum electrodynamics (QED) as a more complete understanding of light. Scientists today know far more about it than I do, but even their understanding is limited. Research and discussions continue.

In our daily experience, we are most aware of only one aspect of light: the visible spectrum. Two amazing organs, our eyes and brain, allow us to see this relatively narrow part of what is broadly called light. Light makes it possible for us to experience the external world. Sometimes we run away from what light illuminates. Sometimes we run toward the illuminated object or person.

There is much more to understand about light, but here is a practical question: "How important is light?" Consider how these people might respond to that question:

- a young child that uses a night-light
- someone who is lost in the woods at night
- someone who has lost power as a result of a storm
- a farmer
- a surgeon

As I began my research, I knew that light was important, and I assumed that life cannot exist without light. My assumption fit my theology. Gary Zank is one of the world's most renowned space plasma physicists. His credentials at the University of Alabama in Huntsville include eminent scholar and distinguished professor and director of the Center for Space Plasma and Aeronomic Research. Here is Dr. Zank's reply to my question, "Is life possible without light?"

> Light isn't necessary for life, although the complexity of the organisms appears to reduce significantly in the absence of light. For example, certain lichens, mosses, and algae are found in completely dark, deep caverns. These primitive plant forms do not rely on photosynthesis but do require water and a temperate environment. So, these forms of life do not require light at all. More complex forms of life (e.g., extremely deep-water fish) do need light somewhere in the food chain if they're to survive even if they live in an environment completely devoid of light.[22]

I stand corrected. Life is possible without light, but it is a type of life that is foreign to human needs and desires.

Darkness

To help us appreciate the importance of light, let's explore its opposite. Throughout history, rulers and other people in power have appreciated the necessity of light. They have, therefore, sometimes used darkness and isolation as a method of interrogation, punishment, or torture. A 2015 report revealed that as little as forty-eight hours of absolute darkness produce measurable effects, such as hallucinations, paranoia, loss of a sense of time, depression, and hopelessness.[23] Humans can exist in darkness for a period of time, but this is far from what we know as life.

In scripture, light is the symbol of purity, goodness, honesty, wisdom, glory, and love. And ultimately, we are taught that "God is light" (1 John 1:5). In contrast, darkness symbolizes everything that is unknown or outside God's values and purposes:

- mysterious or unfathomable things[24]
- brokenness, despair, hopelessness, and misery[25]
- ignorance and unbelief as in lacking spiritual light[26]
- moral depravity, including participation in the deeds of darkness or impure actions[27]
- death[28]
- the reward for those who reject God's invitation to live in the light[29]

Do not misunderstand this contrast between light and darkness. Although darkness may stop us in our tracks, darkness is transparent to God (Psalm 139:12). God is not confused by or threatened by darkness. The Creator is Lord of all creation, including darkness, and he sometimes chooses to use it for his glory (Deuteronomy 4:11, 5:23; Psalm 18:11). Two examples are the plagues God used to free his people from Egypt and the crucifixion of Jesus (Exodus 10:21–22; Matthew 27:45). God can use anything and anyone for his glory, even darkness.

When we are in a terrifying dark place, there is only one thing we desire. I had a serious accident my freshman year in college. While attempting to unstring a bow for a friend in archery class, my hand slipped. The recurve bow recoiled at blinding speed, and the tip of the bow (not the arrow) hit me in my eye before I could blink. In the emergency room, I was asked that famous question, "How many fingers can you see?" I saw nothing but muddy darkness. I was shocked and scared.[30] It was during my months of recovery that I began to read about someone who would become an inspiration to me. Helen Keller (1880–1968) was an amazingly brave pioneer who became the first deaf and blind person to earn a bachelor of arts degree. Speaking of her own experience in the spiritual and educational darkness, she wrote, "'Light! give me light!' was the wordless cry of my soul."[31] Hundreds of millions of people are blinded by the darkness of pain, fear, sin, shame, hunger, abuse, war, hate, alienation, disease, weakness, and depression. They are crying out for light.

By their own decisions or the decisions of others, many people live in ways that seem to embody darkness. I have known a few of these tormented souls. Decades ago, a curious seventeen-year-old started coming to the church youth group I was leading. Our group worked hard to welcome and include him, although he had rough traits and often acted in overtly offensive ways. As I slowly gained his trust, Philip shared about his life in orphanages, in foster homes, and on the streets. He had experienced a level of pain and alienation far beyond my experience or imagination. I eventually noticed an anger in him that simmered below the surface but sometimes erupted. After participating in our group for over a year, Philip disappeared. Months later, I learned that he had been accused of a brutal felony attack. The defense attorney called me as a witness and asked me to share with the court about ways I had experienced Philip's anger. When I sat in the witness stand twelve feet from Philip, our eyes locked. His expression and countenance were cold, blank, and scary. He had been the victim of darkness, but he had made his own choices. He was possessed and trapped in darkness.

On a mission to Russia right after the Soviet Union dissolved, I was introduced to someone who was living in darkness but desperately seeking light. Through sobs she described a painful marriage and the pressure to have multiple abortions. Seeking compassion and counsel, she had seen a priest. He, however, seemed to be repulsed by her story and gave her no reason for hope. Without a path to escape from shame, she was trapped in darkness.

　　　　　　　　JAMES LOFTIN

Randy had a good position in a large company, but for over a decade he had been in open conflict with another leader. Not wanting to fire either person, the company engaged me to manage and attempt to resolve the conflict. One employee seemed repentant and open to change, but my meeting with Randy was quite different. I asked him the same question I asked his coworker: "Is there anything you can do, or is there any resource you have, to help you forgive your colleague?" Randy thought for several moments and replied through gritted teeth, "There is no way I will ever forgive him." Bitterness. Hate. He was trapped in darkness.

You have your own list of friends, family, and acquaintances who have been or are now trapped in darkness of one kind or another. Perhaps you have experienced deep darkness in your own life.

Dark Night of the Soul

Although St. John of the Cross (1542–1591) was perhaps the first to pen the phrase "dark night of the soul," countless people of faith have walked through this valley of the shadow of death. It happened to the likes of King David, Jeremiah, Augustine, Martin Luther, John Wesley, and Mother Teresa. The book of Psalms includes numerous cries from those who were engulfed in the mystery and hopelessness of an emotional black hole. This type of melancholy threatens to destroy life. It is a depression that is linked to a crisis of faith. It feels like abandonment and darkness.

There was a time in my life when darkness almost consumed me. I had cycled down into the bottomless pit of depression and a sense of worthlessness. I knew the facts about God's presence. I knew I was blessed. I knew I was loved. But these and other life-giving facts were shrouded that night as I sat alone. By the grace of God, the dark and downward spiral was interrupted by a phone call from someone who felt called to contact me. I was given enough light to seek help. Through counselors and community, I found a new way to live one day at a time. I don't want or expect to revisit that dark hole again.

The New Testament introduces Paul with words that communicate the great darkness that shrouded him even from an early age. Paul was blessed in many ways, but he was also blinded by a hateful form of ethnocentrism. As a young man (what we might call a child), he consented to and witnessed the murder of Stephen. Later Paul himself participated in murders and abuse. He was in a dark place. This brilliant but broken man finally saw the light. He moved from being a light suppressor to being a lantern lifted high.

Thank God for Light

A type of life is possible without light, but what if the question is "Can there be life on Earth without the sun?" One NASA article reports, "Nothing is more important to us on Earth than the Sun. Without the Sun's heat and light, the Earth would be a lifeless ball of ice-coated rock."[32] Likewise, human life, as God intended it, is impossible without God's light. Thank God for light—for sunshine, moonshine, photons, rays, and the transforming light of God's love.

The first disciples knew little about the science of light and nothing about primitive plant forms or life in the ocean depths. Even the most intelligent humans today do not fully understand light, although we enjoy its benefits every day. Neither do we understand everything about the light nature of God and what it means for us to be the light of the world. We do, however, know enough to be thankful and take action.

One important purpose of light is to illuminate. We shine lights on art so that our eyes can better appreciate the hues and details. Light does not force us to see; it allows us to see. When we intentionally live in a way that helps people notice the beauty of God, we are reclaiming our identity as the light of the world. Our shining points to the One who provides forgiveness, salvation, deliverance, and hope.

Praise God for all the amazing aspects of light. Our hearts leap in adoration in response to God coming into the world to give us light and life. We have been delivered from darkness and enlisted in God's mission of light.

Be the Change

CHAPTER 3: LIGHT AND LIFE

Consider

- ➤ Think of a time when you were forced to deal with darkness. For example, when you lost electricity during a storm or you were camping. What emotions did you and those with you experience?
- ➤ If you have experienced "the dark night of the soul," how did God provide light for you to move forward?

Interact

- ➤ Share about a time when someone led you out of darkness and into the peace of God.
- ➤ Share about a time when God used you in a similar way in someone's life.

Pray

- ➤ Thank the Creator for sunrises, sunsets, rainbows, and the ability to see.
- ➤ Thank God for the ways light has overcome darkness in your life.
- ➤ Pray for a person, family, or group that is consumed with darkness.

Act

- ➤ Education is one way that we can help people move from darkness into light. Name five more ways or methods.

CHAPTER 4

God as Light

Then the man and his wife heard the sound of the Lord God as he was walking in the garden in the cool of the day, and they hid from the Lord God among the trees of the garden. But the Lord God called to the man, "Where are you?"

—Genesis 3:8–9

Highlights

> - To better understand our role as the light of the world, we must explore the nature of God, the Source of light.
> - God takes the initiative and spares no cost in bringing truth and grace to those trapped in darkness.
> - The way God graciously brings light to darkness offers a pattern for the way we can shine as the children of God.

As a young teenager, I once asked my faithful Sunday school teacher Mrs. Brinson, "The Bible has some interesting old stories, but what is God doing today?" I wanted to know more about this God I was being asked to follow. At the time, I didn't realize the significance of my question. As Gregg Okesson writes, "Who God is directly leads to what God is accomplishing in the world."[33] And what God is doing in the world today provides guidance on what it means for us to be the light of the world. To understand the role of the moon, we must study the sun.

One way that Scripture describes God is with the word "light" (1 John 1:5), and the theme of light runs throughout the Bible. Here are a few examples:

> God's creation and valuing of light: "God saw that the light was good, and he separated the light from the darkness" (Genesis 1:3–4).

> The methods God used to assure and guide Israel in the Exodus: "a pillar of fire to give them light" (Exodus 13:21).

> David's testimony: "You, Lord, are my lamp; the Lord turns my darkness into light" (2 Samuel 22:29).

> Zechariah's song: "Because of the tender mercy of our God, by which the rising sun will come to us from heaven to shine on those living in darkness" (Luke 1:78–79).

> Jesus's statements about himself as the Light of the world in John 8 and 9.

> Jesus's statements about his followers being the light of the world in Matthew 5 and John 8.

> Luke's description of Jesus's appearance to Saul on the road to Damascus: "a light from heaven flashed around him" (Acts 9:3).

> John's view of the new heaven and new earth: "There will be no more night. They will not need the light of a lamp or the light of the sun, for the Lord God will give them light" (Revelation 22:5).

God Always Takes the First Step

God is holy, eternal, unchanging, omnipresent, omniscient, loving, merciful, just, and so much more. God's light can be as gentle as a warm sunrise or as overwhelming as a bolt of lightning. One key attribute of God is his gracious decision to always take the initiative. In chapters 1 and 2 of Genesis, we find Adam and Eve enjoying life as they walk with God in perfect communion. The created and the Creator lived in absolute harmony until Adam and Eve believed a lie and used their freedom to make a life-altering choice. Because of their rebellion, Adam and Eve experienced separation from God and the guilt, fear, shame, and darkness associated with life apart from a relationship with the Creator. The next image in this narrative is one of the most surprising storyline twists in the Bible. "Then the man and his wife heard the sound of the Lord God as he was walking in the garden in the cool of the day, and they hid from the Lord God among the trees of the garden. But the Lord God called to the man, 'Where are you?'" (Genesis 3:8–9).

The Father went looking for his wayward children. The Creator walked toward the created. The Holy moved toward the unholy. God called out to them instead of leaving Adam and Eve alone in their sin. It appears that when the Lord beckoned them, Adam and Eve had not had a change of mind or taken one step of repentance. The action they did take—hiding—only further separated them from God. Holy, omnipotent God took the first step. Adam and Eve sat in their sin and shame, but the Creator of the universe moved toward them. This big step was all grace. God loved them too much to leave them in shame and darkness, separated from the Source of life and light.

The Creator of the universe did not wait on an invitation from rebellious Adam or Eve to visit that dark corner of Eden. God saw their need, felt the pain of separation, and embraced them as they were. There were consequences for their sin, but there was also grace. God moved toward them and even made garments to help cover their shame. Although they broke away in pride and selfishness, God loved Adam and Eve. This portrait of God's light and grace gives hope to all of us, regardless of how far we have run from God.

The gracious initiative of God is most clearly seen in the Incarnation. "The people walking in darkness have seen a great light; on those living in the land of deep darkness a light has dawned" (Isaiah 9:2). God took on mortality and came to us offering reconciliation and transformation. God brings us from darkness to light. We celebrate this aspect of God's nature with songs as old as "Amazing Grace" (John Newton, 1779) and as new as "Reckless Love" (Cory Asbury, 2017):

The overwhelming, never-ending
Reckless love of God
Oh, it chases me down
Fights 'til I'm found
Leaves the ninety-nine
I couldn't earn it and I don't deserve it
Still you give yourself away[34]

What Is God Doing?

Here is the answer to the important question "What is God doing in the world?" With gracious, transforming love, God is always moving toward human lostness and suffering. This is a surprising yet core characteristic of our Creator. If you want to find God, to see what Jesus is doing today, find people who are experiencing darkness. That is where God is.

The 2016 movie *Hacksaw Ridge* is based on the true story of a courageous World War II medic, Desmond T. Doss. The movie focuses on the horrendous battle for Hacksaw Ridge on the island of Okinawa in 1945. For his actions, Doss was awarded the Medal of Honor, the most prestigious military award of the United States. The official citation for the medal includes this description: "Doss refused to seek cover and remained in the fire-swept area with the many stricken, carrying all seventy-five casualties one-by-one to the edge of the escarpment and there lowering them on a rope-supported litter down the face of a cliff to friendly hands."[35] According to Terry Benedict's documentary *The Conscientious Objector*, Doss once explained, "I was praying the whole time. I just kept praying, 'Lord, please help me get one more.'" A soldier that survived Hacksaw Ridge said, "It's as if God had his hand on [Doss's] shoulder. It's the only explanation I can give."[36] Desmond Doss was committed to saving lives at any cost.

The Bible introduces One whose commitment to save lives is infinitely beyond the sacrifices of even the most heroic human. Jesus told a story about a shepherd who had one hundred sheep. All but one were safe in the fold, but the shepherd cared about the one. He went after the one (Luke 15:4). Jesus, the eternal Good Shepherd, went all the way to Calvary in order that every sheep, including you and me, might be saved. This is the nature of God. God's sacrificial love and persistent grace give light to the darkness of despair, loneliness, brokenness, guilt, and death that litter the battlefield of human existence.

Let's rehearse this core truth of the gospel. God loves us and wants to be in a life-giving, eternal relationship with us. If you were the only person on earth, Christ still would have died for you.

> ➤ "For the Son of Man came to seek and to save the lost" (Luke 19:10).
> ➤ "But God demonstrates his own love for us in this: While we were still sinners, Christ died for us" (Romans 5:8).

Every story in the Bible, from Noah to Joseph, from Abraham to King David, from the transformation of Saul to the final transformation of all creation, reveals the nature of God. God yearns for us to ask for forgiveness and demonstrate a repentant heart, but God always takes the initiative. It is the nature and mission of light to chase away darkness. Love always makes the first move. Our response of faith is vital but always secondary.

An old worship chorus includes this request: "Open the eyes of my heart. I want to see you."[37] If we want to see God and know God's nature, we can learn much from Christian fellowship, prayer, worship, and the reading of scripture. Theologians speak of the "means of grace" as special acts and observances through which God's children experience the presence of the Lord in ways that transform us. Jesus specifically points to Holy Communion and baptism. God has an infinite number of ways to communicate grace, if we have ears to hear. But there is one means of grace that is often overlooked. I affirm the teaching of John Wesley (1703–1791) about the role of mission and service as a means of grace. God uses of our acts of mercy, our shining in dark places, to transform the world and to transform us. This is part of the meaning of Philemon 6: "I pray that your partnership with us in the faith may be effective in deepening your understanding of every good thing we share for the sake of Christ." Some aspects of God's character and the gospel cannot be fully understood if we only sit in overstuffed chairs clutching study Bibles and highlighters. As moving as worship services and Christian community are, it seems that there are truths that God chooses not to communicate in these settings. God reveals some things about grace only as we stretch ourselves beyond our own cultures and run with Jesus to bless lost and hurting souls. To know more about light and the Source of light, we must join God by entering the darkness millions face every day.

Prodigal Art

In 2002, a bilingual missionary friend and I visited an area in East Asia where few lanterns were shining God's love. As we explored a simple souvenir shop one day, I was shocked by some art that was for sale. There were several large oil paintings with obvious Christian themes: the crucifixion of Jesus, Jesus knocking at a door (a version of *The Light of the World* by William Holman Hunt, c. 1850), and a marvelous portrayal of a wealthy old man embracing what appeared to be his ragged prodigal son.

Through my friend, I asked the merchant if she knew the stories behind these paintings. "Yes," she replied. "They are based on old fables from China's countryside." I smiled, and replied, "I'm sorry, but your information is not correct. I know the ancient stories behind this art. Would you like to hear them?" I expected she might see this as a chance to gain information to help her sell the paintings. At her happy invitation, I briefly shared the good news behind each picture. Saving the prodigal father piece until last, I introduced the old man in the picture as a figure that represents the wise and loving God of the universe. I then asked, "Who do you think the kneeling young person represents?" As she began to speak, I noticed a change in her eyes and voice. Then my friend's translation came through her now shaky voice: "She said, 'That is me.'"

For several minutes, the silence in the shop was interrupted by nothing except the sniffles of three people who were aware of God's tender presence. My missionary friend then continued the dialogue in their shared language as I listened and prayed. After about thirty minutes of interchange, the two women took hands and began to pray. My friend gave the clerk her first Bible as well as the phone number of a Christian in that village. Twenty years later, I still tremble in joy as I remember that bright afternoon. The clerk had no knowledge of or belief in God. She certainly had not asked for this encounter. God had been moving toward her since she was conceived, mostly in ways unnoticed by her. God always talks the initiative.

God's Mission at any Cost

Private Doss prayed, "God, help me get one more." As he prayed, he used all his knowledge, training, and energy to move toward hurting people and carry them to safety. Doss delivered those who were walking in the shadow of death into the light of healing and hope. "God is light" (1 John 1:5). God's gracious nature moves toward hurting and lost persons even before they ask for help. God is always moving toward pain as light always seeks to chase away darkness. God's overarching and unchanging mission is to redeem, bless, and transform all peoples for his glory (Genesis 3:6–9; Luke 19:10). Amazingly, God spares nothing to accomplish this mission. No price is too high. "For God so loved the world that he gave his one and only Son, that whoever believes in him shall not perish but have eternal life" (John 3:16).

God ran to Adam and Eve, to Moses in the bulrushes, to Daniel in the lion's den, and all the way to Calvary. God is still running. Right now, the Spirit is pursuing the abused, the hurting, and those who have never heard the good news. Jesus is running to Afghanistan, to China, to Boston, and to your zip code. God is on the move. It is God's nature and mission to chase away darkness with truth, mercy, and grace.

Be the Change

CHAPTER 4: GOD AS LIGHT

Consider

> ‣ Which of the attributes of God seems most precious to you today?
> ‣ God came looking for you long before you were looking for a Savior. God took the initiative. How does that make you feel?

Interact

> ‣ Share something you learned about God and life as you helped meet the needs of others. For example, what did you learn about God when you gave food to someone who was hungry, served on a short-term mission trip, or told a friend how you began to follow Jesus?
> ‣ Consider the ways that God shines. What does God's shining suggest about the way you should live as the light of the world?

Pray

> ‣ Thank God for caring about all the sheep. Thank Jesus for running all the way from heaven to your zip code.
> ‣ Ask the Spirit to give you a passion like that of Jesus and Private Doss to save lives at any cost. Ask God to help you find and love someone who doesn't feel that God or anyone else is looking for them.
> ‣ Pray for Christians who are shining in places where they could be imprisoned or killed for their faith.

Act

> ➤ Write a note of gratitude and encouragement to a person who sacrificed in some way so that you would be drawn closer to Jesus. Consider people like parents, siblings, teachers, pastors, coaches, coworkers, and friends. Write the note even if the person is already in heaven.

CHAPTER 5

God's Mystifying Method

> The Lord had said to Abram, "Go from your country, your people and your father's household to the land I will show you. I will make you into a great nation, and I will bless you; I will make your name great, and you will be a blessing. I will bless those who bless you, and whoever curses you I will curse; and all peoples on earth will be blessed through you."
>
> —Genesis 12:1–3

Highlights

- ➤ Jesus finds joy in using his imperfect followers to transform lives and the world.
- ➤ It is easy to forget that God has at least two reasons for giving us every blessing in life.
- ➤ "Cruciform discipleship" is a term that describes a response to God's grace that includes praise and allegiance as well as witness and service.

Light changes everything. Light makes plants green and grow tall. Light brings us healing, hope, and guidance. God is light, and he has a beautiful and intricate lighting system that is changing the world. The Apostle James refers to God as "the Father of the heavenly lights"

(1:17). Commenting on this statement about God's eternal identity, Christopher Wordsworth (1807–1885) wrote,

> God is the Father of all lights—the light of the natural world, the sun, the moon, and stars, shining in the heavens; the light of reason and conscience; the light of his Law; the light of prophecy, shining in a dark place; the light of the gospel shining throughout the world; the light of apostles, confessors, martyrs, bishops, and priests, preaching that gospel to all nations; the light of the Holy Ghost shining in our hearts; the light of the heavenly city; God is the Father of them all. He is the everlasting Father of the everlasting Son, who is the Light of the world.[38]

Take a minute to recall some ways the Father of lights has changed and is changing your life and the lives of people you love. Every transformation is beautiful and unique. God's light comes to us in diverse ways that at times may seem random. Scripture, however, suggests that God's work is always

- consistent with God's nature,
- driven by grace,
- focused and intentional,
- in response to human need,
- aligned with God's preferred future for creation, and
- for the purpose of bringing God glory.

The mission of God is to redeem, bless, and transform the world with the light of truth and grace. That mission is as amazing as God's method is surprising. God's mission is infinitely larger than the Church's, but we have an important role in God's transforming work. Lesslie Newbigin (1909–1998) commented on this strategy of God as "a fact of inexhaustible significance that what our Lord left behind Him was not a book, nor a creed, nor a system of thought, nor a rule of life, but a visible community."[39] Warren Cole Smith and John Stonestreet call this "God's audacious plan to change the world through everyday people."[40] As children of God, we are the children of light and partners in God's light mission. Most of God's attributes are far beyond the ability of mere mortals—such as omnipresence. But other aspects of God's nature are made possible to redeemed sinners empowered by the Holy Spirit. As the light of the world, we can shine like God shines, albeit like the moon instead of the sun. Irenaeus (130–202) wrote this about the Church's ministry: "The faithful are called through grace to be partakers of God's holiness (Hebrews 12), restored to their primordial capacity to reflect, like a mirror, the radical holiness and purity of God, even though their mirroring is always imprecise."[41] Almighty God has chosen you as a partner in the ongoing mission of light.

Blessed to Be a Blessing

In a world where change is a constant and often unnerving aspect of life, I take comfort in the fact that there are at least three things that do not change: God's character, God's mission, and God's method for achieving this mission. One snapshot of God's method is found in Genesis 12. God says to Abraham: "I will make your name great, and you will be a blessing" (v. 2). Then God adds, "all peoples on earth will be blessed through you" (v. 3). Not unlike Jesus's words that identify his disciples as the light of the world, God's statement to Abraham is both a promise and a challenge. God will bless Abraham and all who trust in God; we will be a blessing to people far beyond our imagination. This is an Old Testament version of Jesus's words in Acts 1:8.

We have all received countless blessings from God. If you stop to name a few now, you may want to sing a song of praise and gratitude. But consider this important question: Why does God bless you? If you answer too quickly, you may miss a vital truth. God has at least two reasons for blessing us. Yes, God's gifts are signs of love, but there is more. God has blessed you with resources, talents, and gifts for a purpose beyond your own enjoyment. We are blessed to be a blessing to others. The same was true for Abraham. When we allow our blessings to pass through us to others, we bring God glory, honor, and renown. Psalm

106:7–8 describes how God delivered the Israelites "for his name's sake, to make his mighty power known." The Lord of creation has chosen to bless and use people as fallible as us to bring light and transformation to the world.

Transformation

Let me be clear about my use of the word "transformation" here and throughout the book. My use of the word is related to the biblical words "salvation" and "blessing." I use "transformation" to communicate the diverse and wonderful ways Jesus Christ impacts lives and the world, both spiritually and temporally. When a person responds in faith to God's invitation, he or she is transformed from darkness to light, from alienation to membership in the family of God. God's Spirit continues the work of transformation by shaping us day by day into the people we were created to be. This aspect of transformation includes blessings like forgiveness of sins, restoration of relationships, and healing from all types of brokenness. Jesus transforms lives (see 2 Corinthians 3:18, Romans 12:2, 2 Corinthians 5:17).

God's transforming work in the life of a believer also includes the creation of a desire to bless others. Although we were once alienated from God, through Christ we became the children of God and happy ambassadors of Christ. Moved by the Spirit, Christians seek to love our neighbors as an expression of our love for God (Luke 10:27). This love naturally pushes us to find ways to meet the needs of people and to invite them to trust in Jesus. In communities where Christians love and pray like this, things begin to change. More people experience unconditional love as needs like hunger, housing, and education are addressed. Trust is built. Hope grows. More people trust Jesus. God transforms lives and communities.

The biblical portrait of God includes a concern for the eternal as well as temporal condition of humankind, although all suffering will not be remedied until Christ returns in glory. In the meantime, Christ followers are called to shine in such a way that the maximum number of people may see Jesus and be transformed by God's grace.

Spotlighting Jesus

As we allow God's blessing to flow through us, our words and actions reflect God's love and glory in a way that causes onlookers to consider the Source of light. William T. Cavanaugh describes the Church as "a sacrament, a material form through which God is seen—a window to God."[42] Our sins and brokenness may at times mask the Lord's glory and light, but the presence and glory of God abide in us. God uses our love-in-action to alert observers that there is more going on than can be explained by mere human kindness. Moved by the Spirit, people—even prior to belief in God—can sense God's presence, light, and glory.

The goal of our shining is to draw attention to the Savior and bring glory to God (Matthew 5:16). A vignette from a short-term mission trip to Costa Rica illustrates the relationship between our shining and God's glory. I was trying to keep our team calm although the airline agent seemed uncertain that our luggage had been loaded onto the plane that would take us home. When I pushed for more assurance, he smiled and motioned for me to follow him. To my surprise, he took me through doors marked "Authorized Personnel Only," down stairways, and out onto the airport tarmac. When we reached the plane, the agent hopped onto the moving conveyor belt and motioned for me to follow. Once inside, he pointed at a pile of bags and asked, "Is this your luggage?" It was indeed. The team of Americans applauded wildly for the agent when I shared the news. They knew that I had done nothing but communicate the good news. They knew that their savior was the agent, not their trip leader. I had no authority to go onto the tarmac or get inside that plane. I had no power to get our luggage to the United States. I had one thing: a relationship with one with power and authority. Only the agent deserved glory. All I did was make his work known, somewhat like the moon reflecting the light of the sun.

To rehearse, we shine so that others may see God more clearly and decide for themselves how to respond—"… that they may see your good deeds and glorify your Father in heaven" (Matthew 5:16). Light does not force anyone to see; it allows us to see.

A Feast for One

God's mystifying method of using people as the light of the world is both amazing and risky. Although we have been saved by God's gracious light, we still tend to be self-centered. Consider this fable:

> Once upon a time, the van of a tour group broke down in a remote area. There was no cell phone service and little water or food. Assuming that rescuers would soon arrive, the travelers relaxed and chatted. Minutes turned into hours and stomachs began to rumble. After twelve hours, the whining voices grew loud with hunger and a growing fear. When dawn broke on day three, spirits were at rock bottom. As they discussed their options, hope reignited as they saw someone approaching. Cheers and applause began to rise and the newcomer waved in appreciation. The growling stomachs, however, were focused on the large paper sack he was carrying and the Styrofoam containers peeking out of the opening.
>
> At that moment, the travelers caught a whiff of the aroma of barbecue. Barely restrained by politeness, they pressed in on the visitor and his sack. They believed their prayers for rescue and nutrition had been answered, but then the man held up his greasy hands and asked for calm. His next words shocked the group.
>
> "A kind benefactor gave me a huge sack of barbecue to bring to you. She knew you would be hungry. I realized that also, but I couldn't help myself. Barbecue is my favorite food, and I was hungry. I'm sorry but I finished off the entire sack just before I found you. God blessed me with this food because he loves me. I am praying for you, and I'm sure God will eventually bless you also. Hallelujah." As he walked away, he shouted over his shoulder, "Remember, God loves you and I do too."

There are several things wrong with this picture, but here's the core. It's easy to enjoy and thank God for our blessings without considering how those blessings might flow to others. The "Prayer of the Sheep" (Psalm 23) is one of many passages that help us remember the intended flow of our blessings. Toward the end of David's song are these words: "You prepare a table before me in the presence of my enemies. You anoint my head with oil; my cup overflows" (v. 5). Part of what the passage celebrates is the way God provides for us. The Good Shepherd gives us more than we need. The anointing and the overflowing cup communicate the extravagance of God's blessings. One reason that God overfills our cups is so we will have enough to share with enemies and others. We are blessed to be a blessing.

As God's children, we have two equally important dynamics always at work in our lives: our relationship with Jesus and our participation in his ministry in the world (Matthew 22:37–40). Paul Chilcote, my former colleague on the faculty of Asbury Theological Seminary, referred to this bidirectional approach to life as "cruciform discipleship." The vertical line in the cross reminds us of the interaction between holy and loving God and the children of faith. God reaches down to us in grace, and we respond in faith, confession, praise, and allegiance. The horizontal line in the Cross reminds us that joining God in mission to lost  and hurting people is vitally connected to authentic faith. Without the horizontal axis of the cross, the form is merely a big "I"—a symbol for a life characterized by selfishness. This cruciform concept is helpful as a construct to draw attention to the often-overlooked service aspect of our calling. A more circular construct is breathing. As we inhale, we receive God's grace and respond in allegiance and worship. As we exhale, we share and demonstrate God's grace. This, too, is an act of worship. When we unconditionally love our neighbors as we love ourselves, we are demonstrating our love for God. Our witness, service, worship, prayer, and fellowship can intermingle and overlap in ways that change the world and bring God great delight and glory.

William Booth, the founder of the Salvation Army, echoed the truth found in James 1:27 regarding our vertical and horizontal response to grace. Booth wrote, "I have ever felt that true religion consists not only in being holy myself, but in assisting my Crucified Lord in His work of saving men and women."[43] Joining the family of God is likewise a decision to join God's ministry on Earth. Yes, divine blessings flow to us because God loves us. And, yes, divine blessings flow to us in order that we might bless others with God's great love. This understanding of God's nature and our calling may be clear, but that doesn't mean our response is easy or without obstacles.

Let the Waters Flow

God graciously rains blessings down on us, but we are not the ocean, the endpoint of the flow of blessings. We are rivers that receive blessings and keep them flowing downstream toward others. This "river life" does not come naturally to us. It is easy to dam up the river of blessings with our selfishness, greed, and fear. Our natural inclination is to eat or store an overflowing sack of barbecue that could have blessed many others.

Sadly, history is full of instances where Christ followers did not let God's blessings flow through them to others. I could give a thousand examples from my own life. Here is one: As a sophomore at Millsaps College, I was sitting in a hallway with other students, waiting to enter class. Startled by a door slamming, I looked up and saw my friend Bob entering the hall. He rushed past me with an intense look on his face, but he didn't speak to me. Before reaching the exit at the other end of the hall, he turned around and began to slowly walk back the way he came. Bob's hands were raised chest-high with palms out communicating "easy now." Only then did I realize that Bob had been fleeing another man. As the distance between them decreased, Bob began to calmly speak: "Hey, let's just talk about this." As they came together, the pursuer quickly grabbed a chair and broke it on Bob's shoulders as he crouched in a defensive posture. I don't remember what happened after that. But this image has stuck with me. My friend was under attack, and I did nothing. I could have yelled, prayed, pleaded, or otherwise sought to diffuse the emotion. I had options and abilities, but I was frozen by fear and selfishness.

I have failed to act or responded slowly many times when I have perceived a need. I continue, however, to ask God to give me grace and courage to not be trapped as a spectator when action is necessary and I have resources to share. Psychologists have a term for this hesitancy: "the bystander effect."[44] The presence of other onlookers during an assault or other crisis makes it less likely that an individual will intervene. When there are many onlookers, intervention is even more unlikely. A crowd of witnesses somehow lessens our determination to take action even when we have resources. With today's technology, millions of eyes watch disasters unfold in real time. Our best response to many needs may be prayer, but there are crises that we have the ability to impact with some type of action, and yet we remain bystanders.

In response to the rise in anti–Asian American harassment in 2021, organizations began offering "bystander intervention and de-escalation training" events.[45] The emergence of these programs reminded me that we all need tools to help us determine how to respond when a need is screaming in our faces. As Christ followers, we know that we are the light of the world, and we want to shine, but in the heat of the moment, it is easy to be paralyzed. In addition to injustice and physical abuse, pains like hunger, homelessness, and ignorance of God's grace surround us. When faced with an opportunity, inaction is often a failure to pass on the blessings God has entrusted to us. Addressing the darkness of inequality in 1965, Dr. Martin Luther King Jr. called the children of light to repent from paralyzing fear and apathy.[46] When God's people are silent or frozen bystanders in the face of suffering, we place baskets over our lanterns. We fall short of what the Father of light intends for the children of light. The causes of this failure to shine are as diverse as fingerprints, but all of them are anchored in selfishness. J. Herbert Kane linked this limitation of our shining to misplaced priorities: "After the second or third generation, Christianity tends to take on cultural overtones, and soon its members begin to take their heritage for granted and lose all desire to share their faith with friends and neighbors. The churches turn inward on themselves, and soon their chief preoccupation is their own survival, not the salvation of the world."[47]

Note that this is just a tendency; it is not unavoidable. We don't have to let our fears, selfishness, limitations, or the bystander effect overrule God's calling. One of the wonderful roles of God's Spirit is to help us remember and live out the priorities of God. The Spirit in us can overcome any tendency to turn inward. The Spirit moves and empowers us to bless others as we are blessed. The Spirit gives us an attitude of adventure about shining near and far. The Spirit opens our eyes, gives us courage, and moves our feet to turn outward in response to the needs of the world. The Spirit makes it possible for us to lift our lanterns high.

It is a challenge to continuously refuse to dam up God's flow of blessings with our selfishness. It is relatively easy to lapse into a spectator response to the needs of the world. We have the Spirit and the Word, but disciples, families, churches, and organizations need reminders. We need partners. A tactical plan and a system of accountability will greatly increase the likelihood of success if we want to be like Abraham—a conduit of God's blessings, a river of life, and a lantern lifted high.

Flawed Lanterns Shine Even More Brightly

Jesus refers to his followers as the light of the world, but we are imperfect, needy, fallible, frail, mortal, sinful, selfish, weak, and foolish (1 Corinthians 1:27). The Lord is perfect and does not need help, but God has chosen to use the imperfect to bless humankind. God uses ordinary people like you and me to do extraordinary work. It is a mystery, but both the fact of God's redeeming grace and the method God has chosen to shine in the world bring glory to the King of kings.

Entering the Sistine Chapel in Vatican City, visitors are blown away by the beauty and scope of the art. Michelangelo masterfully illustrates nine stories from Genesis, including the creation of Adam and a depiction of the hand of God reaching out to Adam. If I get to see it someday, I imagine that I will not be too surprised by the beauty of the art. I already know the abilities of Michelangelo, and I have seen other examples of his brilliance. If someone, however, showed you this art and told you that the creator was a child or a sight-impaired person, you would be astonished. You would have questions like: "Who is the artist's teacher?" and "How did she accomplish this?" Finally, you might gasp: "I thought only an artist like Michelangelo could create something so beautiful." This example highlights the genius of God's decision to use imperfect and underqualified children of faith as mission partners. Jesus alludes to this truth as he addresses his followers who might have been doubting the success of their movement if Jesus was no longer present. "Very truly I tell you, whoever believes in me will do the works I have been doing, and they will do even greater things than these, because I am going to the Father" (John 14:12). Paul declares that God uses fragile humans in order to reveal "that this all-surpassing power is from God" (2 Corinthians 4:6-7).

Another snapshot of Jesus's life seems to suggest that God's use of imperfect women, men, and children was more than a tactical decision. God has joy in using people like you and me. After the seventy-two disciples report to Jesus about their missionary trips, Luke reports, "At that time Jesus, full of joy through the Holy Spirit, said, 'I praise you, Father, Lord of heaven and earth, because you have hidden these things from the wise and learned, and revealed them to little children. Yes, Father, for this was your good pleasure'" (Luke 10:21). Our active partnership with Jesus brings God pleasure. When we lift our imperfect lanterns high, God smiles.

No Big Deal

When we intentionally participate in the mission of God, we are not doing something unusual or unexpected. We are simply living up to our name. We are the people of God, Christ-followers, coworkers in God's mission to spread the gospel of Christ (1 Thessalonians 3:2). We are the light of the world. Shining is not something to be considered strange or even commendable. Consider my encounter with a porter in a Malaysian hotel. When I offered him a tip for helping with my bags, he seemed confused. Finally, he realized what I was attempting to do. He began shaking his head, and with a wide smile, the porter said, "No, no, no. It's my job." This reminded me of Jesus's words in Luke 17:10: "So you also, when you have done everything you were told to do, should say,

'We are unworthy servants; we have only done our duty.'" We are the people of God, the light of the world. Charles Van Engen's description of our job in God's strategy is profound: "'The Church is a marvelous, mysterious creation of God that takes concrete shape in the lives of the disciples of Jesus as they gather in local congregations and seek to contextualize the gospel in their time and place.' He went on to say that when we reach out in mission, we become in fact what we already are by faith, 'God's missionary people.'" [48]

Jürgen Moltmann's trinitarian view of mission keeps this focus: "It is not the church that has a mission of salvation to fulfill in the world; it is the mission of the Son and the Spirit through the Father that includes the church."[49] We are partners with God. We are the light of the world. We shine by blessing others as we are blessed. We shine the brightest when our words and deeds match the concerns and methods of God. This shining is exciting, but in a sense, it is not a big deal. It's who we are. It's our job.

Four Characteristics

As we do our job as the light of the world, we will discover ways to shine for God in keeping with our own gifts and the opportunities God provides. My witness in the world may not look like yours, but our shining must be rooted in God's nature and purposes. Here are four general characteristics of faithful shining:

1. **Loving.** We love and bless others as God loves and blesses us. Unless our words and actions are motivated by a love for God and a love for our fellow humans, they are useless (1 Corinthians 13:1). There is no shining apart from love.
2. **Holistic.** Although we may sometimes have to separate proclamation and demonstration, our concern matches that of Jesus. The salvation and spiritual health of people are the ultimate concerns, but Jesus cares for the whole person. (Matthew 4:23).

3. **Global.** In addition to serving in our own zip code, our shining seeks to impact the lives of people that have a language, race, religion, income, education, and geography far different than ours (Acts 1:8).
4. **For God's glory.** Regardless of the type of service we provide, our overarching driver is for God to receive glory. The moon always praises the sun.

Every time you participate in God's mission, every time you demonstrate cruciform discipleship, every time you bless others with the blessings God has given you, and every time you remember your identity and choose to shine brightly, God has joy. That's enough to get you fired up about living missionally every day. The song "People of God" reflects on 1 Corinthians 13 and calls us to remember who we are as the Church of God.

> We could see blind eyes opened
> Know all the mysteries of our faith
> We could sing all the highest praise
> But if we don't have love
> We're left with nothing
> People of God rise up
> Rise up and shine God's love
> We are the light of the world. [50]

By faith, you received God's gracious gift in Jesus, and you are seeking to serve and please him. You sing with King David: "The LORD is my light and my salvation" (Psalm 27:1). As part of your response to God's grace, you want to be a faithful part of God's mystifying method of blessing and transforming the world. Even as the Lord spoke to ancient Israel, you have heard this challenge and promise: "I will also make you a light to the nations" (Isaiah 49:6 GNT). More than you have imagined, your life can communicate grace and bring solutions that change the world for God's glory.

Be the Change

CHAPTER 5: GOD'S MYSTIFYING METHOD

Consider

- ➤ Think about God's decision to use the Church—and you in particular—as a partner to transform the world. What other strategies might God have chosen?
- ➤ How does God's invitation to shine make you feel?

Interact

- ➤ Share five blessings God has given you.
- ➤ Brainstorm with each other about how each blessing could be overtly used to bless others, near and far.

Pray

- ➤ Consider some aspect of your life that seems limiting—perhaps a bad decision or a health, family, or financial issue. Ask God to show you how this aspect of your life could be used to bless others.
- ➤ Pray for churches, seminaries, and organizations that are inspiring, equipping, and mobilizing people to serve in God's mission.

Act

- ➤ Consider the four general characteristics of faithful shining: loving, holistic, global, and for God's glory. In what ways do your service and witness demonstrate these values?
- ➤ What is one thing that you can do this week to better align your shining with these values? Take at least one step forward and share your decision with a friend.

CHAPTER 6

Light Mission Status

See to it that you complete the work you have received in the Lord.

—Colossians 4:17

Highlights

> By clarifying the meanings of terms, we can more accurately see the status of our mission to shine.

> Although there is much to celebrate, current statistics and trends reveal that our mission is not complete, our efforts are often less than excellent, and something needs to change.

> An honest progress report provides insights for future planning, which lead to greater mission success.

The invitation of Jesus to "Come, follow me" is a bidding to salvation and so much more (Matthew 4:19). It is an invitation to walk with Jesus and live like Jesus. We are God's children, disciples, and partners in a mission to announce good news and transform lives by the grace of Jesus Christ. The Church has been running with Jesus in this mission for two thousand years.

A greeting that I often use with friends is "How's it going?" In this chapter, I want to put our efforts to shine for Christ in context by asking the friendly question "Church, how's it going?" The *team progress report* is a tool commonly used by business, education, and industry leaders. It is an evaluative process that provides a picture of how well a team has completed a project or assignment. A progress report can

- ▸ provide clarity and get all team members on the same page;
- ▸ facilitate greater collaboration among team members;
- ▸ improve transparency and accountability, highlighting actions to celebrate and areas to improve; and
- ▸ provide insights for future planning toward greater success.

This chapter attempts to provide a team progress report on the Church's mission of light. It will clarify key terminology, note some successes, identify some areas of underperformance, and restate the urgency of addressing underserved needs. The purpose of this progress report is to provide guidance and stir up enthusiasm for our participation in God's mission. This review of statistics and trends will also underscore our potential impact as we follow Jesus "in the midst of a crooked and perverse generation, among whom you shine as lights in the world" (Philippians 2:15 NKJV).

What Does Our Sent-ness Mean?

By this point, you may have decided that this is a missions book. Depending on your definition of that word, your assumption could be grossly incomplete. This book is about following Jesus. I am writing about the core of our faith. Shining is not an optional or peripheral activity, as is sometimes associated with the term "missions."

The role of the Church in the world is directly related to God's character. The mission of God includes things that are far beyond the scope of the Church, but we are an important part of God's movement to redeem and transform the world. In principle, we may understand this statement, but what does this look like in real life? What actions and ministry are included in this important aspect of what it means to be Christ followers, people of faith, the Church? Before we explore the status of the light mission God has given the Church, let's agree on some key terminology.

Although the responsibility of sharing and showing God's love to others is dynamically connected with our identity as God's children, the word "mission" rarely occurs in the Bible. The English word comes from the Latin noun "*missio,*" but the parallel Greek word used in the New Testament is "*apostellō,*" which means "to order (one) to go to a place appointed."[51] This is the biblical basis of the English words "mission," "send," and "apostle." "*Apostellō*" is the word used when Jesus reports that God sent him (Matthew 10:40) and when Jesus sends out the apostles two by two (Mark 6:7). At the core of the original meaning and traditional interpretation of "*apostellō*" is this concept: God sends people of faith from where they are to a place of God's choosing in order for them to communicate the good news of Jesus Christ. For example, the church at Antioch sent Saul and Barnabas to Cyprus to do the work God called them to do: "preach God's Word" (Acts 13:1–3). Jesus's call in Matthew 28:19-20 contains these same core elements: God's authority, God's grace, the sending, the going, and the proclaiming—all with the goal of making disciples.

> Then Jesus came to them and said, 'All authority in heaven and on earth has been given to me. Therefore go and make disciples of all nations, baptizing them in the name of the Father and of the Son and of the Holy Spirit, and teaching them to obey everything I have commanded you. And surely I am with you always, to the very end of the age.'

At some point in history, this passage became known as the Great Commission. It has often been seen as a key text for understanding the mission of the Church.

Over the decades, however, confusion has developed as to the meaning of the "sent-ness" or mission of the Church. The definition of terms and the areas of focus continue to change. A survey of US churchgoers in 2021 found that less than half were familiar with the term "Great Commission."[52] Although this may only indicate that other terms for mission are being used in some sections of the Church, the researchers at Barna think otherwise. "Overall, there is a slipping awareness of the missional calling of the Church at large."[53]

As Keith Ferdinando and others have noted, there are several factors in this migration of definitions and emphasis. First, there is a growing and appropriate understanding that communicating God's good news (evangelism, preaching, making disciples) is not the only thing Christ followers are sent to do. Loving our neighbors as ourselves certainly involves an effort to relieve the temporal as well as spiritual forms of suffering that plague our neighbors. Second, cultures have become more accepting of various kinds of diversity—including non-Christian faiths and the rejection of faith. This gracious attitude is appropriate, but there is a side effect. The concept of evangelism today is often held with suspicion, and many believe that it "is not a necessary, perhaps not even a desirable, function of the church."[54] The Barna Group reported in 2019 that almost half of Christian Millennials (47%) in the United States "agree at least somewhat that it is wrong to share one's personal beliefs with someone of a different faith in hopes that they will one day share the same faith."[55] I understand the pushback of many toward evangelism, especially given the forceful, disrespectful, cold communication styles some believers have used. In reality, these harsh styles of witness have nothing to do with the model of Jesus or the instructions of the Bible: "Always be prepared to give an answer to everyone who asks you to give the reason for the hope that you have. But do this with gentleness and respect" (1 Peter 3:15). Sharing the good news in gracious ways remains as one of the key responsibilities and joys of Christ followers.

A third reason for confusion regarding our "sent-ness" and the mission of the Church is the nonreligious use of the word "mission." Think of how often you read or hear about the mission statements of companies, schools, and churches. This secular but important use of the word further clouds the Christian understanding of "sent-ness." Lastly, words like "mission" are too often seen as departments of the local church, a special calling for super-Christians, or certain extracurricular activities for normal Christians. Consider the organization of your local church's ministries. It may not have a missions department, but it probably has a focus area with a label like "outreach," "service," "compassion," "mercy," or "global ministries." Ultimately, the label is not important. The activity represented by the label is, however, vitally important, as it refers to the core identity of Christian disciples and not just a department of a church. For these and other reasons, the meaning of the word "mission" has become fuzzy and often unhelpful as a term to describe the work of the Church.

This book is focused on Jesus's use of the word "light" to describe the ministry of Christ followers. Our values and the way we shine must be related to the values of God and the complex and dark aspects of human suffering. In her treatment of John Wesley's concept of "complicated wickedness," Christine Pohl explains the brokenness of the world as the "intertwining of several fundamental problems: the absence of true religion, a deep social alienation, degradation and oppression, and acute physical need."[56] In view of the complex needs of our fellow pilgrims on earth, Gregg Okesson calls Christians to refuse simplistic answers and to "thicken" our witness by addressing the holistic needs of people.[57] As I encourage Christians to lift our lanterns high, I am referring to the broadest understanding of the mission of the Church. I see no wiggle room in scripture for an either-or definition. A faithful witness gives attention to the Great Commission and as well as to what has been called the Great Commandment (loving God and our neighbors, Matthew 22:37-39). The Lausanne Movement states, "There is no biblical dichotomy between evangelistic and social responsibility."[58] I also appreciate Ray Bakke's down-to-earth observation: "Christians are the only people who can truly discuss the salvation of souls and the rebuilding of city sewer systems in the same sentence."[59] C. René Padilla refers to these two aspects of our mission as the "two wings of a plane."[60] God has sent us to shine on Earth by moving forward on the wings of proclamation and demonstration, evangelism and service, disciple-making and justice.

I am not sure that this is a helpful question, but some ask, "Is proclamation or demonstration the priority?" Ajith Fernando calls for caution in this discussion. While our ministry strategies may vary, the Church "must press on in its vital mission of bringing the mercy of God to the world, the most crucial aspect of which is bringing the greatest news the world has ever known, the gospel of Christ, to the ends of the earth."[61] In a similar way, Keith Ferdinando urges the Church to not forget our "primordial and unconditional responsibility to make disciples ... Definitional ambiguities must not be allowed to obscure the absolute centrality of that vital task."[62] As the light of the world, it is our joy and responsibility to shine in ways that demonstrate mercy as well as offer an invitation to a saving relationship with God through Christ Jesus by faith.

In the Church's ongoing struggle to clarify our mission, God has used people like David J. Bosch (1929–1992) to encourage us to move beyond a programmatic understanding of missions as the spreading of Christianity or church expansion to a broader and more biblical understanding of the Church participating in the mission of God (*missio dei*).[63] Bosch ends his book *Transforming Mission: Paradigm Shifts in Theology of Mission* with this summary and definition: "Mission is quite simply, the participation of Christians in the liberating mission of Jesus wagering on a future that verifiable experience seems to belie. It is the good news of God's love, incarnated in the witness of community, for the sake of the world."[64]

I am indebted to writers and leaders like these because I did not always have this both/and understanding of God's priorities. For years, I was almost totally preoccupied with proclamation. I focused on evangelism and discipleship. Unfortunately, I probably thought those involved in mercy ministries were less mature than I was, using their time in less important ways. By God's grace, I eventually moved beyond that sad plateau. The witness of wise leaders, an increasing appreciation for scripture, the crushing realities of life, and the inner testimony of God's Spirit moved me to a broader and more biblical understanding of what it means to be the light of the world.

Your Definition of "Mission"

With this background, let me ask you to reconsider your definition of "mission," "being sent," "outreach," "shining," or whatever term you want to use. How do you define the work of the Church in the world and your work as the light of the world? If your definition seems to be heavy on one end of the proclamation–demonstration continuum, take time to think more deeply. Review what scripture says about compassion, grace, healing, deliverance, proclamation, charity, evangelism, and making disciples. Over the years, I have helped dozens of congregations rethink their understandings of our role in God's mission on earth. Here are a few definitions they developed:

- Endeavors that reach beyond our families and barriers of distance, culture, economic status, and language to fulfill the Great Commission and the Great Commandment.
- Ministries that cross social and cultural boundaries to demonstrate the hope, healing, and love of Jesus Christ to lost and hurting people as part of God's plan to make disciples for the transformation of the world.
- Any effort that reaches beyond the needs of our family, friends, and congregation for the purpose of fulfilling the Great Commission and the Great Commandment by proclaiming the gospel of Jesus Christ, making disciples, and relating to the whole need of humankind.
- The proclamation and demonstration of the love of Jesus Christ culturally near and far.

Your definition may be similar or quite different. Whatever words are used to describe this partnership, our method and motivation must be faithful to the nature of God. There is no one correct definition of our calling, but the process of sharpening your understanding by reading God's Word, thinking, discussing, and praying will bring you clarity and new passion as you seek to shine brighter as the light of the world.

A Progress Report

As we gain a better understanding of terms and the scope of our light mission, we can more clearly see our progress in achieving the mission. "Hey Church. How's it going?" How are Christ followers impacting the world? Questions like these are not new. In Acts 11 we learn about the response of the Church leaders in Jerusalem to news of great ministry results in Antioch. Barnabas was sent to check out the reports. "When he arrived and saw the evidence of the grace of God, he was glad and encouraged them all" (11:22–23). The disciples in Jerusalem must have had some type of metric for determining ministry success. In this case, they were curious to see if the reported conversions of Gentiles were authentic according to the Church's definitions. Like Barnabas, my desire is to accurately review and graciously encourage the work of the Church. To get a helpful progress report on the status of the Church as the light of the world, I asked two questions:

1. How has our performance matched our job description?
2. What progress have we made toward the goals assigned to us by the Owner?

There are many beautiful moments in the history of God's Church where Christians have lovingly and sacrificially served hurting people, respectfully invited people to consider God's love, and transformed communities with grace and hard work. Your own local church may be growing, and many of your friends may have recently begun a journey with Jesus. Perhaps hundreds of orphans, widows, and other disadvantaged people are being blessed and empowered by God's people in your city. Light is overcoming darkness. In his 2020 book *A Public Missiology: How Local Churches Witness to a Complex World*, one of the churches Gregg Okesson celebrates is the Africa Brotherhood Church in Machakos, Kenya. Okesson highlights the congregation's response to the practical needs of the people with programs of agriculture, education, and health care, as well as creative approaches to evangelism. People are coming to Christ, and the society is being transformed. These and a thousand other examples throughout history compel us to shout, "Hallelujah." God is using the Church. It is wonderful when our performance matches our job description.

If we only focus on the Church's bright moments, we bypass a critical part of the process and miss some of the benefits of an authentic report on our progress. Seeing the performance of the Church with rose-colored glasses is likely to create mission-drift and a status quo attitude toward our role in the world. Speaking the truth in love, it is necessary to admit that there have also been and continue to be times when the actions of those identified as Christians are an embarrassment to the cause of Christ. The Church has sometimes yielded to the temptation to ignore our "sent-ness" or to engage in the mission in a way that dishonors God. Sometimes our response to God's call has been less than our best. Sometimes it has been blatantly sinful, not unlike the offering of Cain, on which God "did not look with favor" (Genesis 4:5). The depravity of the world and the besetting sin of selfishness continue to distract Christians from our core calling.

It is beyond our ability to fix people or cultures. God alone is redeemer and liberator. Our role is to diligently announce the goodness of God and give our best to meeting temporal needs as partners in God's mission. The amount of darkness and pain that is not being addressed by the Church is evidence that our task is unfinished and our execution is less than excellent. Consider these snapshots:

> Although millions are believing in Christ every year, the percentage of people who identify themselves as Christian is decreasing. The percentage increased for nineteen centuries and then plateaued:
  o   AD 100: 0.45%
  o   AD 1000: 16.94%
  o   AD 1900: 34.46% (highest)
  o   AD 2000: 33.02%[65] (The percentage of Christians in 2018 remained at 33%.)[66]
> Of the 7.7 billion people in the world, 3.2 billion, or 41.6%, are considered "unreached." This term describes people who are part of an ethnic or people group which has no indigenous community of believing Christians with adequate numbers and resources to evangelize their group without the assistance of Christians outside their group.[67] Most of these people have not had a chance to hear the good news for the first time.
> One in five people (over a billion souls) are waiting for the Bible in their first language—the language they best understand. Approximately 7,360 languages are spoken in the world, but

complete translations of the Bible are available in only 704 languages. Translation of the Bible for 171 million people, speaking 2,115 languages, has not even started.[68]

> 822 million people are chronically undernourished today, up from 785 million in 2015.[69]

> 736 million people, almost 1 in 10 people in the world, live on less than $1.90 a day. Nearly one half of those living in extreme poverty are children.[70] To put this number in perspective, a person with an income of $25,000 a year in the United States lives on $68.49 a day.[71]

> 2 billion people have no choice but to use a source of drinking water that is contaminated with feces.[72]

I hope you didn't skim over those staggering statistics. Each number is a person created in the image of God—a soul so precious that God's Son submitted to the Cross for them. Review the numbers again.

Our stewardship of God's resources includes far more than our bank accounts. How we invest our dollars, however, says much about our priorities and the accuracy of our understanding of the world's needs. The statistics below relate to how churches invest funds entrusted to them, but I expect the giving of individual Christians might have a similar breakdown.

> A 2007 review of how churches invested their funds revealed that 87% is for ministry with people who are already Christian, 12% is for work with people who have been exposed to the gospel but are not Christians, and 1% is for work with the unevangelized and unreached people.[73]

> An analysis of church giving in 2017 revealed that a weighted average of about 2¢ per dollar was used for international missions.[74]

> A 2019 survey indicated that churches invested 7.7% of their budgets in ministry to people beyond their congregations (international mission 4.2%, domestic mission 3.5%).[75]

> A 2020 report found that "American Christians spend 95% of offerings on home-based ministry, 4.5% on cross-cultural efforts in already reached people groups, and .5% to reach the unreached."[76]

Empty Tomb, Inc. has tracked and analyzed the ways churches have supported missions since 1968. Their data suggest that it is common for the focuses of churches to turn inward, allocating an increasing percentage of their resources on the congregation itself.[77] This sounds like another example of what J. Herbert Kane identified as the tendency for churches to become preoccupied with their own survival to the exclusion of God's greater calling.[78]

Time to Change

These numbers are less than exhaustive, some are dated, and definitions may not be consistent. Most of the victories of God's children go unnoticed by human eyes and are not included in statistical reports. The statistics I have shared, however, are precise enough to point to general trends. Churches invest a small percentage of their finances and energy in people who have urgent needs that are not being addressed by other Christians. In terms of light, we tend to lift up our lanterns in rooms illuminated by many other lanterns.

I am eternally thankful for the work of the Church throughout the ages. I am the recipient of the faithful ministries of countless men, women, and children. I am in no position to, and have no desire to, judge the Church. I have deep gratitude that mercy triumphs over judgment (James 2:13). My comments in this chapter are intended to be a status report on our progress, not a judgment of that progress. We need an honest picture of the Church's progress and current trends to know where and how to shine faithfully today and tomorrow. The wisdom of novelist, poet, and civil rights voice James Baldwin (1924–1987) applies to the way the Church responds to God's calling and the needs of the world: "Not everything that is faced can be changed, but nothing can be changed until it is faced."[79]

If we were to apply the statistics above to a road where you and I might live, it would look like this: There are nine homes on our road. The people in each home have similar strengths, needs, desires, and challenges. Each resident has dignity and is valued by God. You and I live in one of the three homes that have light (electricity, warmth, and modern technology). Three homes farther down the road have seen the light from our homes, but they are wary of it. According to their traditions, light seems strange. The final three homes are much farther down our road—so far that we usually forget that they are there. These families have neither heard of nor seen light other than that from the sun, moon, stars, and fire. We don't know whether they would like to have more light or not. They've never been given this option.

God invites people who live in homes with light to consider this obvious question, "How shall we share the light that has been given to us?" Paul urged Archippus to "complete the work [he had] received in the Lord" (Colossians 4: 17). Likewise, we are called to complete our assignment as the light of the world. We are blessed to be a blessing. We are invited to do our best that all might experience the forgiveness, peace, healing, and hope found in the light of God's love.

To summarize, God has done marvelous things through the Church, but a massive number of urgent needs are not being addressed, and millions languish without knowledge of Christ. After reviewing a list of statistics similar to what I shared, David Platt said, "We face two options. We can retreat from this mission into a land of religious formalism and wasted opportunity, or we can risk everything to fulfill the divine purpose for which we have been created. And I say let's risk it all."[80] God's mission has not changed. Our calling has not changed. Our desire to make a difference has not changed. Something, however, needs to change about our attitudes, our approaches, our focus, and our urgency.

Remember that one outcome of an honest progress report is insight for future planning and greater mission success. The next three chapters can be used as a progress report for your own life and witness. These pages will help you more clearly understand the dominant way you respond to God's blessings and share God's light with others. This self-evaluation is the next step in reclaiming your identity as the light of the world.

Be the Change

CHAPTER 6: LIGHT MISSION STATUS

Consider

> ‣ According to your *job description* as a partner in God's mission, what kind of progress report will you give yourself? Be real but kind.

Interact

> ‣ Share which aspect of shining you rely on the most— proclamation or demonstration. Explain.
> ‣ Which of the statistics about the Church's impact is most disturbing to you?

Pray

> ‣ Thank God for the ways your church and the Church are meeting needs.
> ‣ Ask God to help your church leaders focus more on underserved and unreached people and needs.
> ‣ Pray for researchers and other behind-the-scenes workers who provide information that can guide the Church in shining where light is most needed.

Act

> ➤ Write down the first names of five people who probably have not given their lives to Christ. Pray for them to see and receive the light of God's love.

CHAPTER 7

Selfish Light

If anyone has material possessions and sees a brother or sister in need but has
no pity on them, how can the love of God be in that person? Dear children,
let us not love with words or speech but with actions and in truth.

—1 John 3:17–18

Highlights

- ➤ God has made us the light of the world and given us the freedom to decide how brightly we shine.
- ➤ Christ followers fall into one of three categories according to their dominant responses to God's blessings: selfish, benevolent, or strategic.
- ➤ We have the tendency to focus most of our prayers and energy on ourselves and those closest to us.

God's decision to use imperfect people like you and me is outrageous and exciting! The Almighty has invited us to engage in something with eternal significance. We are the light of the world, but God has given us the freedom to choose how we shine. You can be a lantern lifted high or a lamp that provides almost no light beyond your own home. Refusing darkness is not the same thing as shining brightly.

The first disciples certainly felt honored, as well as anxious, when Jesus called them to follow him. Three years later, imagine how they felt when he commissioned them to be witnesses to the ends of the earth. Upon his ascension, Jesus left the mission in their hands. The first disciples stumbled forward as they graduated from watching to doing. Eventually they graduated from a real but naive faith limited by their own power and ethnic identity to a transcultural faith made possible by the presence of Christ in their lives. The impact of their shining continued to increase. This is the path that every growing disciple can expect, but not all experience it.

My research, reflections on my own faith journey, and deep discussions with Christians around the globe have convinced me that Christ followers fall into one of three categories according to their dominant responses to God's blessings. People are selfish, benevolent, or strategic. The light shining from one's life is either dim, bright, or brilliant. People who place their lanterns under a basket are on one end of a continuum. They share light only with their close network of family and friends. On the opposite end are Christ followers who are intentional about lifting their lanterns high to impact lives across the street and around the globe.

Wild Ones

Before you began reading this book, you may have finished the phrase "born to ___" with a word other than "shine." Some would fill in the blank with the word "run" as a nod to the sport of running or the 1975 song by Bruce Springsteen. Others would use the words "be wild." The band Steppenwolf's most famous song, "Born to be Wild," remains a mainstay of culture and has been covered by bands such as U2, Etta James, and Bruce Springsteen. Commenting on the lasting appeal of the lyrics, Steppenwolf's lead singer John Kay said, "Every generation thinks they're born to be wild and they can identify with that song as their anthem."[81]

Mr. Kay's statement is theologically correct. All of us, as fallen creatures, are born wild. The Creator, however, has a plan to move us from being wildly selfish to being wildly loving toward God and our fellow humans. When filled with the redemptive light of God, we become the light of the world. Because of the freedom God has given us, however, we maintain the ability to make choices about how we live and shine. In Galatians 5, Paul cautions Christ followers about using their freedom to yield to our selfish, sinful nature. The apostle uses the words "selfish ambition" in his description of a life opposed to God's character and calling (19–21). We are born wild and selfish, and that tendency continues even after we find freedom in Christ.

Individualism

Although selfishness has influenced the focus of all humans since the bad choice of Adam and Eve, there are unique cultural pressures on some of us. Individualism is an historical plank in the culture of the United States. There are beautiful aspects of this philosophy. It can foster creativity and the initiative to move beyond outdated and inadequate beliefs and tactics. It also affirms the value of each individual—a concept rooted in the Christian belief that all people are created in the image of God. But there is a dark side of individualism. The French philosopher Alexis de Tocqueville (1805–1859) described individualism as "a kind of moderate selfishness that disposed humans to be concerned only with their own small circle of family and friends."[82] Unchecked individualism can degenerate into alienation, divisiveness, entitlement, narcissism, nationalism, elitism, and racism. You and I are all too familiar with the pains related to individualism and selfishness.

Individualism pours gas on the fire of our tendency to be self-centered, but there are also broader, transcultural factors that push us toward a preoccupation with *me, mine, and ours*. Charles Taylor, author of *A Secular Age*, and like-minded philosophers refer to the premodern Church (prior to the seventeenth century) with words like "organic," "holistic," and "integrated." In that age, all things—worship, ministry, economics, politics, work, relationships, education, birth, disease, and death—were held together by one's faith in and cooperation with the transcendent, all-powerful God. As the modern era began, this unified, integrated understanding of life and God began to fall apart, and the culture became mostly anthropocentric and egocentric. Commenting on Taylor's writing, David Kern asserts that this secular or modern mindset "values, above all, individual choice and, indeed, the ability to make of God what one wills."[83] Views of faith, life, and God have shifted and continue to shift in ways that can distract us from our core calling to be the light of the world. Addressing this calling to bless others, Shane Claiborne commented, "It's very countercultural because everything in the world is pulling us away from the pain, away from the suffering. But the entire story of Jesus is about a God who is moving near to the pain."[84]

As you consider how you want to participate in God's mission, it is wise to acknowledge that there are internal and external voices that urge us to selfishly keep our lanterns low. Sometimes these voices are blatantly in opposition to the values and reign of Jesus. But often the whispers are subtler and can easily be misinterpreted as guidance from a heavenly messenger (2 Corinthians 11:14). None of these spurious tongues, however, has the power to keep you from shining brightly.

The Selfish

In my model of shining, the first of three categories is the selfish. These people accept God's blessings but ignore God's calling to bless others. In a futile search for meaning and joy, the selfish allocate most of their resources to the enjoyment of life and the hope of a secure future for their family and close friends while demonstrating little interest in those outside their network. David F. White describes it this way: "While we are created in God's image, made for joy and restless in its pursuit, in our modern consumerist world our quest for joy is interrupted by our endless grasp for momentary, transactional, and idolatrous fun."[85] Part of the reason some people have this skewed focus is their tiny frame of reference. They have tiny worlds, tiny Bibles, and tiny understandings of what it means to follow Jesus. They don't see the needs of others and tend to evaluate the status of the world through an egocentric filter:

"If my world is okay, then the world must be okay." Like the people described in Genesis 11, the selfish are content to build towers that honor themselves instead of their Creator. Although this portrait is rather dark, many trapped in this style of living maintain an outward appearance of politeness, professionalism, and religious zeal.

In the parable of the rich fool (Luke 12:16–21) Jesus contrasts two styles of living: that of the selfish person who stores up things only for himself or herself and that of the person whose relationship with God is characterized by generosity. Jesus calls us to a lifestyle that is the opposite of selfishness. Being "rich toward God" in generosity is not easy. Sharing our blessings with another person is an act of faith. There may come a time in the future when I need the item I gave away. This is part of the significance of the animal sacrifices required in the Levitical law. The law directed worshippers to offer animals without blemish (Leviticus 1:3). The offspring of a flawless animal would most likely have the traits of their parent, such as size, speed, and resilience. These offspring would increase the likelihood of the herd being healthy and decrease the chance that the owner's family would go hungry. By offering this animal without defect to God, the worshipper said, "I am trusting God more than anything I can see or control." Offering gifts to God in worship and sharing our possessions to bless others are acts of faith. This is wisdom overcoming foolishness, generosity conquering selfishness.

Although the selfish may have moments of generosity, this is not their dominant style. Their attitude toward the needs of others is self-imposed ignorance and detachment. They think little about the potential impact their blessings might have on the world. They separate faith in God from the ethical lifestyle of the Bible. The selfish are guilty of the accusation leveled at Moses Shapira, a dealer of antiquities in Jerusalem in the eighteenth century. A critic wrote that Shapira may have "converted to Christianity but not to good works."[86] A selfish life is only partially converted.

In Luke 9:23–24, Jesus offers a hard word to anyone considering his call. "Whoever wants to be my disciple must deny themselves and take up their cross daily and follow me. For whoever wants to save their life will lose it, but whoever loses their life for me will save it." Jesus calls us to surrender control of our lives. An understanding of this verse and countless others suggests that the term "selfish Christian" might be an oxymoron.

Vampires

I have a confession to make. I was a vampire, and sometimes I relapse into my old bloodsucking ways. Dallas Willard has defined vampire Christians as those who say something like this to Jesus: "I'd like a little of your blood, please. But I don't care to be your student or have your character. In fact, won't you just excuse me while I get on with my life, and I'll see you in heaven?"[87]

When I responded in faith to the grace of God, Jesus cleansed me of all sin, wiped away my shame, and launched me on a journey of faith, service, and witness. But I sometimes fall back into the self-centered thoughts, words, and actions that dominated my pre-Christian days. Don't get me wrong; I'm not talking about those nefarious behaviors that make headlines. I'm talking about a selfishness and a preoccupation with all things that I might consider "mine"—my family, my friends, my work, and my stuff. It is easy to grasp a gift of God in a way that distorts the biblical priorities of Christ followers. Think of a two-year-old in a tantrum shouting "mine" as his mother tries to persuade him to share his toy with a friend.

Several years ago, I noticed that almost all prayer requests that others and I shared in Christian meetings dealt with issues directly related to the life of the person making the request. There is nothing wrong with asking for prayer for my job, my health, my mother's care, my friend's child, or even my dog. But if these types of needs consistently dominate my concerns and prayers, a misalignment with the priorities of Jesus is revealed. My prayers have sometimes sounded like "Dear Jesus, bless me, my family, and my friends. Thanks. Bye." That is not the prayer of someone seeking to shine brightly for God's glory.

This kind of discipleship hardly honors Christ or furthers his mission in the world. The selfish demonstrate a caricature of discipleship in which religious people try to suck blessings out of the Savior while continuing to live by their own interests. There are many examples of how the selfish reveal their loyalties. In restaurants, waiters often grimace when they serve a table of folks who arrive for lunch after a church service. It is likely that this table will be demanding and cheap, more likely to leave a Bible verse than a decent tip. Politicians or business owners who loudly identify themselves as Christians sometimes seem to be using religion as a marketing tool. A person in the selfish category might spend more effort trying to be perceived as pious than they do actually being faithful by serving, blessing, and welcoming others.

Encouraging Selfishness

Christian seminaries, preachers, teachers, musicians, and authors may unintentionally feed our tendency to be selfish. A philosophy known as the prosperity gospel blatantly feeds a self-centered approach to life, but the prosperity prophets are not alone. A subtle encouragement of selfishness occurs across the spectrum of theologies and denominations. The words used in many invitations to trust Christ promote a "Jesus and me" lifestyle: Just believe and God will bless you with forgiveness, peace, heaven, and a church family with good food and free childcare. These promises may be valid, but they highlight only a portion of the covenant between the Creator and the created. The emphasis is on the blessings a convert will receive and not on the cost of discipleship.

Perhaps you can relate to the conundrum a friend of mine once described: "I go to three Bible studies each week. I'm also in a sharing group, and I have a devotional time every day. I go to worship services at least weekly, and I'm constantly reading Christian books. Inspirational emails and messages hit my phone before I get out of bed every morning. So why do I feel like I'm missing something?" Several years ago, my sister Kathy described her spiritual life with similar words and then sighed, "All I do is eat. I rarely exercise. I'm just a fat Christian."[88] It is easy to allow our Christian life to be defined by our own lives—me, mine, and ours—as we remain uninterested in the needs of those outside our own networks. Expressing a measure of incredulity over divorcing one's true faith in God from a faithful response to needs around us, Martin Luther (1483–1546) wrote, "It is impossible, indeed, to separate works from faith, just as it is impossible to separate heat and light from fire."[89] The Apostle James asserts that faith and deeds are vitally connected, and our actions are somehow used by God to perfect or complete our faith (James 2:20–23). When we underappreciate or ignore the horizontal aspect of the faith (addressing the spiritual and temporal needs of others), we are as selfish as any vampire in a Hollywood film.

Nothing New

This selfishness is nothing new. Part of God's indictment of ancient Israel was a response to their selfish motivation for worship and obedience. "You have said, 'What's the use of serving God? What have we gained by obeying his commands or by trying to show the Lord of Heaven's Armies that we are sorry for our sins?'" (Malachi 3:14 NLT). The selfish questions are still popular today: "What's in it for me?" "How can I benefit from obeying God?"

We all want God's blessings, but we can be hesitant if not stubborn in responding to the responsibilities that accompany God's blessings. Consider Jonah's response to God's calling to proclaim good news. Instead of going to Nineveh, Jonah fled in the opposite direction. The people at Nineveh were immoral, abusive, and evil. Believing that he was better than them, Jonah tried to escape God's call. He knew God was gracious and feared that the Lord would forgive the Ninevites and not destroy them as they deserved. Jonah's self-righteousness and self-centeredness kept him from obeying God's calling. Our own biases, prejudices, and selfishness can likewise keep us from following God's call to serve others, even those who seem to be far outside our circle of niceness. If we intentionally flee from God's calling, we would be wise to heed the warning of my friend Josh Womack. Commenting on Jonah and the whale, Josh cautions all who are tempted to avoid God's calling to service to "stay away from all large wildlife."[90]

Grace Must Lead Us Somewhere

Few of us may flagrantly disobey God's call like Jonah, but all of us deal with selfishness on a daily basis. Philosophically, a dichotomy between love for God and love for others seems impossible, and yet it happens. That is why the Bible often addresses our selfish tendency. "If anyone has material possessions and sees a brother or sister in need but has no pity on them, how can the love of God be in that person?" (1 John 3:17–18). I want to be a man who always runs toward God, accepts God's blessings, and pursues God's calling to share those blessings with excellence. I pray that selfishness will not lure me to hop a ship heading in the wrong direction. I want the love of Christ to move me beyond selfishness to servanthood. I want to be faithful to my family and friends, but I also want to join God's mission to lost and hurting people beyond my circle of intimacy and comfort. I don't want to be a vampire. I don't want to be spiritually fat. I affirm the way Billy Still describes our calling to follow Jesus: "The grace we receive, beautiful as it is, must lead us somewhere. If it is to live, it must lead us to lives of generosity."[91]

When Christ enters a life, we miraculously become the light of the world, and yet sin and the curves of life can affect the brightness of our flames. The lamps of selfish Christians are held low. The illumination may be enough to keep them from stumbling, but few others benefit. If my description of the selfish fits your life, don't despair. You don't have to stay on that vampire ship sailing in the wrong direction, and you need not question God's love. The Savior of the world loves you just as you are, but he desires to save you from selfishness. God wants to help you shine much brighter than you imagine.

I don't know whether many Christ followers fit in the selfish category, but I have met many good people who probably fit in the next category.

Be the Change

CHAPTER 7: SELFISH LIGHT

Consider

- ‣ As a disciple of Jesus, are you expecting to grow and improve in the way you shine as a partner in God's mission?
- ‣ Why is that your expectation?

Interact

- ‣ In what circumstance is your selfish vampire persona most likely to make an appearance?
- ‣ Whom do you know that has moved from selfishness to a lifestyle that is dominated by kindness, respect, and grace?
- ‣ How is that transition coming along in your life?

Pray

- ‣ Thank God for the many opportunities to worship you enjoy.
- ‣ Ask Jesus to deliver you from selfishness.
- ‣ Pray for pastors and worship leaders as they design services that are cruciform, balancing worship with a call to witness.

Act

- ‣ Write down ways that you can refuse selfishness this week. Consider the ways you pray, spend your time, use your money, and use your voice.

CHAPTER 8

Benevolent Light

So watch your step. Use your head. Make the most of every
chance you get. These are desperate times!

—Ephesians 5:15–16 (MSG)

Highlights

- ▸ Busyness, traditions, lack of knowledge, misplaced values, and other factors make it easy for good Christians to settle for lifestyles that are far short of our potential as partners in God's mission.
- ▸ The various seasons of life influence how we respond to the needs of the world. Our challenge is to do the best we can at any given stage.
- ▸ The Good Samaritan pushed beyond benevolent living and is a model of shining with excellence.

In previous generations, the faces and cries of suffering people around the world have been mostly hidden. As dark as life might have been in one community, the residents did not also suffer with knowledge of the pain distant others were facing. Technologies developed in the past fifty years changed all that—cell phones, the internet, and social media. Ignorance, therefore, is no longer an excuse for inaction. William Wilberforce spent his life bringing the darkness of slave trade into the light in seventeenth century England. Speaking to leaders he had recently exposed to the horrors of human trafficking, Wilberforce said, "You may choose to look the other way, but you can never say again that you did not know."[92]

The statistics in chapter six may have opened your eyes to the degree of darkness in the world, but the digital screens in your life have already revealed the faces and cries of masses. The question now is regarding your response. How does this awareness of suffering and lostness intersect with your awareness that God has invited you to shine? If your primary response to God's blessings and the world's needs is not selfish, you must either be benevolent or strategic. The benevolent category is made up of truly good-hearted people. They care. They want to make a difference. Their decisions are usually not self-serving. These brothers and sisters are often active in their faith and serve in their communities. The lanterns of the benevolent provide light, but far below their potential. Deep down, they know this. Many of these folks long to get their lights higher. Others are oblivious. Others are content.

The word "benevolent" is often used to describe someone who is active in or disposed to doing good. One might comment, "Roger is a benevolent businessman." The word can describe an organization that has the purpose or reputation of doing good or serving people. The antonym is the word "malevolent," which refers to the disposition to do ill. Linguistically, the bar for being described as benevolent seems to be quite low. A benevolent person is more likely to have good wishes for others than to have ill wishes. Often, however, there is a vast canyon separating one's benevolent wishes for those in need and one's tangible steps to meet those needs.

As we continue to explore these three ways people respond to God's call to shine, I want to be sensitive to the variety of life situations we all experience. I have no desire to create false guilt. Our involvement in God's mission is absolutely influenced by the different stages of life. We go through seasons when factors like health, family dynamics, pressing temporary work requirements, and restrictions enforced by our countries of residence impact the way we shine. On one level, I understand and affirm the lyrics of "Dream Small," sung by Josh Wilson:

Dream small
Don't buy the lie you've gotta do it all
Just let Jesus use you where you are
One day at a time
Live well
Loving God and others as yourself
Find little ways where only you can help. [93]

I have concerns, however, about our tendency to camp out in this land of small dreams. For me, this is a temptation to return to vampire living. My colleague Laura Messina, mother of three small children, has spent most of her adult life actively reaching out to people overseas as well as to international students God brings to the United States. Consider her reaction to the philosophy voiced in "Dream Small": "I am in a season of having to be content with living much smaller than before. I feel like it's OK to tell someone who is in a season like me, but who clearly wants to do more, that it's OK to engage where you are. But for people who aren't looking beyond themselves, this philosophy can be an excuse to stay there."[94]

Our dreams of shining can remain large, although faithful involvement in God's mission will have different looks in the different stages of our lives. In the year we both turned sixty-five, my friend Billy reminded me of our need to always put faithfulness and success in context. He referred to his first ultramarathon after heart surgery to make an important point: "With a damaged and weakening heart, I will never be as fast as I was at thirty-five … I will be and do what I can in the context of my body and life."[95] Context is key. Circumstances change. Our abilities change. But our dreams, desires, and commitment to shine brightly don't have to change. Our challenge is to do the best we can at any given stage in our life. To be satisfied with anything less is to have a type of gratitude for God's blessings that is less than complete.

Jeff Foxworthy has made a ton of money by playing off the line

"You might be a redneck if ..." Borrowing from his style of speech, I invite you to contemplate the following snapshots of the benevolent. Please note my use of the words "might be." Each statement below is an opportunity for you to consider a good aspect of your life that may not be fully developed. Allow this list of stereotypes to be a mirror that helps you examine your stewardship and the ways you are responding to God's invitation to shine brightly.

You might be benevolent if you volunteer to help poor people during the holidays.

In early November each year, families and church groups around the United States begin to ask this question: "What is our holiday project this year?" This tradition can be a beautiful and biblical act of kindness. But the benevolent have little or no involvement with poor or disadvantaged people the rest of the year. The underlying motivation for their benevolence may be related to continuing a tradition or easing guilt about their own wealth. This lifestyle is certainly not evil, but it is not a generous lifestyle characterized by ongoing efforts to bless others as God has blessed us.

You might be benevolent if you serve others because it teaches good lessons to your children.

A family in our church once called me on Christmas Eve with this request: "Can you find us a needy family? My wife and children want to bless some children who won't have many presents tomorrow." All the ministries I knew were closed and had already made arrangements for their clients, so I encouraged my friends to wait a few weeks. In January, there would be an abundance of unmet needs. I later learned that the family had dropped off a carload of new toys outside the locked doors of an inner-city community center. The underlying motivation for the benevolent may be the enhancement of certain family values as much as if not more than a desire to meet the needs of others. I'm not judging that motivation. Ministry efforts can sometimes achieve more than one purpose. But something is askew in the heart of the person that helps others only if the action also meets a need in his or her own family.

You might be benevolent if you are involved in many good causes.

There are innumerable needs in our communities and the world. Churches, community organizations, and social media bombard us with calls to action. To maintain positive relationships with those making the requests, the benevolent offer a little time or money to almost everyone who makes a request. The chief motivation for the benevolent may be to save face and make other people happy. This unfocused approach can dilute our joy in serving as well as the impact of our investments of time and money.

You might be benevolent if you give cash to beggars.

It has happened to most of us. Someone asks you for help as you encounter him or her on the sidewalk or at a traffic intersection. Many times, the easiest thing to do is to give cash. This response may sometimes be appropriate, but more often, it is destructive. Other responses may be more effective in meeting the actual needs of the person, but they involve preparation, time, or risk. The benevolent don't even consider ways to address the real needs of the person, and they feel a level of satisfaction that their cash gift may have helped someone.

You might be benevolent if you participate in short-term mission trips.

I love short-term mission adventures and have led almost a hundred. On these brief service trips, team members feel blessed by the gratitude and friendship of those being served. It feels good to give testimonies and provide manual labor. The unity of the team is strengthened, and each member is brought closer to God. All of these are good things. The benevolent, however, rarely question the impact of the dollars and hours, and once they return home, their serving does not continue. A desire to receive, not serve, may be the primary motivation of the benevolent who go on short-term trips.

You might be benevolent if you believe ministry is mainly done by pastors and super-Christians.

The benevolent decline most invitations to serve, especially those that involve sharing the gospel and serving cross-culturally. They believe that this work is for professionals and zealots. The benevolent may pray, send encouraging notes, and cheer wildly for those who serve, but they are rarely involved in ministry themselves. The roots of their inaction may be fear, insecurity, poor theology, or common selfishness. Their excuses often sound like "I'm not good at serving and I'm too busy anyway. But I am very thankful for those who can serve." The benevolent underestimate what it means to be the light of the world.

You might be benevolent if you think faithful stewardship is demonstrated only by the donation of money.

The sharing of our finances and possessions is part of faithful stewardship, but we all have other blessings and resources that can be leveraged for the kingdom—time, influence, relationships, hobbies, and more. The benevolent miss opportunities to make maximum impact by failing to consider nonfinancial ways to shine. People who push beyond the limitations of benevolence consider ways to use all their blessings to bless others. Wallace was a senior pilot for a major airline. When his schedule included China, he often asked me whether there was any kingdom work that he could do on his trip. Sometimes he delivered Bibles to pastors. On other trips, he would meet with Christian workers to pray with and encourage them. Wallace's profession made it possible for him to shine where many others can't. Wallace is a good steward of all his resources, not just his money.

You might be benevolent if you ask God to use you where you are.

Many Christ followers faithfully reflect God's light on their families and communities. The benevolent ask God to help them be a loving witness at their school or business, and God answers these beautiful prayers. God uses us where we are, but God is also concerned about needs far beyond my zip code. God brings people to us so we can bless them, but he also sends us to people. Even if we don't travel to distant lands, we can pray for needs in those places and look for other ways to bless the people. The benevolent, however, are content to shine only in their local area. The benevolent do many good deeds, but the recipients of their generosity are relationally or geographically near. They shine, but not very far.

You might be benevolent if you desire to do good in the world but your expectations are low.

Some people are content with helping a few starfish survive. They will not entertain grand ideas about saving thousands or creating solutions that address root causes. When faced by passionate souls seeking to change the world, the benevolent silently label them as naive zealots. The benevolent lack the faith to believe that God can and does use his children of light to bring major transformation to lives, communities, and nations. The benevolent dream small.

You might be benevolent if you find solace in comparing yourself with your peers.

My perception that I am a better witness or steward than another Christian will give me false joy and contentment. Even if I compare my current shining to my previous ways of shining, I will not have adequate information to evaluate my faithfulness. The most helpful way for measuring faithfulness has nothing to do with our peers or our history. The question is "How am I responding to God's call today?" The benevolent seek to serve at a level that is better than their past efforts or better than their peers' instead of being motivated by God's worth to give their very best. Rephrasing a line from Jim Collins, being good or benevolent is often the enemy of doing great things for God.[96]

You might be benevolent if you are patient.

Imagine that you are on a sinking ship. Trying to fight off shock, you force yourself to answer one question: What action you should take?

Shall you paint the deck or sing hymns of faith? A day earlier, these might have been perfectly good things to do, but they are not the most important activities in light of your current situation. Those activities do not match the urgency of the need. The benevolent may rush to do many things in their lives, but when it comes to shining, they are patient—too patient. They want to help people, but they respond to God's call as if the needs of their community and the world are not significant or urgent.

You might be benevolent if you do the same good deeds every year.

It is easy to get into a pattern of shining that is convenient and predictable. The benevolent are the ones who advocate repeating last year's charitable service because "We've always done it." I mostly agree with the adage "When something isn't broken, don't fix it." Needs, technology, and tactics, however, change frequently. The benevolent are content with repeating a project or donation ad nauseum because they feel in control, it fits in their calendars, and they enjoy it. Responding to this tendency, Scott Moore asks, "Is our addiction to convenience destroying our ability to follow Jesus?"[97] Although simple research may show that there are more pressing needs than those that were addressed last year or there are more efficient methods to address those needs, the benevolent are not fond of research. They are fond of continuing traditions and doing what is convenient.

You might be benevolent if you are successful.

The Bible often gives specific cautions to those who are rich, well-educated, powerful, healthy, and otherwise blessed in the world. All these gifts are from God, but they can create a slippery slope when it comes to the stewardship of life. Speaking of the call of the Christians to be agents of change in our broken world, Francis Chan addresses a common barrier to our shining. We are successful "at things in life that don't really matter."[98] The question to be answered is not "Are you successful?" or "Do you make donations to worthy causes?" or "Do you invest time to help others?" The important question is "Are you doing your best to use your resources in ways that transform lives and bring God glory?"

You might be benevolent if you are retired.

Although the concept of retirement is unthinkable for most people in the world, it is a season of life that some long for and plan for. Retiring from a career is one thing; retiring from being a good steward who shines brightly is another. Paul Heinz writes about the difference between living life as a continuing story and living life as epilogue.[99] Like a book that ends with a chapter titled "Epilogue," when the benevolent reach the chapter in life called "Retirement," the active narrative of their life story stops. They are content to coast until they die. Retirement can be an excuse to not shine very brightly. Paul Baddour, however, is following a different path. Due to God's sovereignty and Paul's wise decisions, he retired from active corporate work at age forty-six. At that point, he could have coasted into epilogue and let younger folks do the heavy lifting of Christ's light. Paul could have used his time and money to love his family while continuing to worship regularly, tithe, and be a good witness to his neighbors. Paul does all that and more. At age seventy-six, Paul is continuing his story of blessing the world. Every day, he celebrates light and confronts darkness in prayer. Every week, he spends hours coaching and encouraging boards of ministries, as well as individual missionaries. Lifting the light of Christ doesn't look the same for Paul at age seventy-six as it did when he was forty-six, but he is still serving Jesus with great impact. The story of Paul's life continues. The benevolent, however, start coasting as their hair turns gray even if in earlier decades they shone brightly.

What's Your Score?

How many of the snapshots of the benevolent sound familiar? I believe that most people in this category have tender hearts and a desire to shine that drive them to meet needs and bring glory to God. The question before you now, however, is "Are you reaching your full potential as the light of the world?" Perhaps most people continue to live benevolent lives because they don't realize that there is another way. Some move into this lifestyle as a result of a life circumstance like illness, grief, a new baby, a family crisis, or a financial setback. Even after the season of life passes, people fail to move beyond benevolent living. I offer these snapshots of the benevolent in the hope that God might use them as a mirror and a stepping-stone to help you to move beyond the limitations of the benevolent.

The Strategic Samaritan

One of Jesus's best-known parables is found in Luke 10:25–37. Among other things, this parable points to a style of shining that is far beyond the limitations of benevolent living. An expert in the Jewish law recognized that the law and Jesus called him to love his neighbor, but he had questions similar to ours. He wanted clarity. We stand with this legal expert and ask Jesus, "Who is my neighbor, and how should I love him or her?" Jesus then shared about a man who was mugged on a well-traveled road. Two religious men passed by but neither stopped to help. Did they even offer a prayer for the man? The third passerby, a Samaritan, stopped and went far beyond the vampiristic behavior of the two religious professionals, and he also refused to stop at benevolence. All three passersby would probably have said that they loved the man, but notice how the Samaritan "proved" his love. Jesus could have ended the story by saying that the Samaritan stopped, gave the man some cash, and prayed for him. This ending would still have been quite a contrast to the behavior of the other two passersby. But Jesus carefully explains how the Samaritan loved the victimized brother by providing long-term, thoughtful, generous assistance that transformed the man's life. The Samaritan took a risk. He moved beyond racial, religious, and ethnic stereotypes. He loved his neighbor as himself. Jesus included the details of the elaborate assistance the Samaritan provided as a statement about faith and love. The Samaritan pushed beyond benevolent living and is a model of excellence. He lifted his lantern high.

The benevolent have a casual attitude toward the needs of others and the mission of God. This attitude produces a very limited amount of light. I generally believe people do the best they can with the knowledge they have. But I have a question for you. It is the same question I would ask a boy throwing back a few starfish at the beach. Do you want to make a bigger difference in the world? In response to Jesus's invitation in Matthew 5, do you want to lift your lantern higher? The urgent needs of the world and the glory of God compel us to live in a way that has more intentionality and impact than selfish or even benevolent living. This is certainly part of the Apostle Paul's challenge: "So watch your step. Use your head. Make the most of every chance you get. These are desperate times!" (Ephesians 5:15–16 MSG). In the following chapter, I'll discuss an approach to life that I call "strategic living."

Be the Change

CHAPTER 8: BENEVOLENT LIGHT

Consider

> ▸ Think about the major stages of your life. Are there aspects of your current situation that make shining for Christ more difficult than it was five years ago?
> ▸ Will it be easier or more difficult five years from now?

Interact

> ▸ Share which examples of benevolent living seem to fit you.
> ▸ Share which examples make you want to tell the author, "Yes, but …"
> ▸ What is the overall problem or limitation with the way the benevolent shine?

Pray

> ▸ Thank God for loving you just the way you are even as grace pulls you closer and closer to who you were created to be.

- ➤ Ask God to give you the eyes, heart, and wise generosity of the Good Samaritan.
- ➤ Pray for Christ followers who are trying to free people from the darkness of human trafficking, abusive relationships, addiction, and depression.

Act

- ➤ Choose one of the examples of benevolent living that fits you. List three ways you can twist that tendency into something that shines brighter.

CHAPTER 9

Strategic Light

Our people must learn to devote themselves to doing what is good, in order to provide for urgent needs and not live unproductive lives.

—Titus 3:14

Highlights

> The strategic are intentional about using God's blessings so that the maximum number of lives are transformed.
> The strategic are driven by the urgency of the needs of people and the desire to honor God with excellence.
> Strategic living is not something that we must do for our salvation. It is, rather, a choice related to our love for our Savior and our desire to please him.

According to the words of Jesus, we are the light of the world. Although we are born to shine, the effectiveness of our lamps varies from person to person and from day to day. According to their dominant response to God's blessings, some people are selfish and others are benevolent. But there is another way. Living strategically is our faithful response to the invitation of Jesus to put our lamps on a stand so that others "may see your good deeds and glorify your Father in heaven" (Matthew 5:14–16).

Strategic living flows from an intentionality to be the best possible steward of God's blessings in order that the maximum number of lives are transformed and God is honored.

The English word "strategy" was originally a military term, but the concept is now used in contexts like business, education, and Christian ministry. Simply put, a strategy is a plan to achieve a desired goal. Goals are not met through hope alone; intentionality and focus are required. Every strategy involves research, resource allocation, planning, and execution. In this book, I use the word "strategy" to refer to the choices a person, church, or group makes to use resources to achieve a vision believed to have been given by God.

Confident and Enthusiastic

Strategic Christians know who they are in Christ. They celebrate their identity as God's children. They claim Jesus's statement "You are the light of the world" (Matthew 5:14). They humbly acknowledge their role in God's mission of light. They affirm the priesthood of believers and reject any notion that clergy or other professional ministers are the true or even most important workers in God's mission. They see shining as an exciting challenge and adventure. The strategic have counted the cost and know that their lives might be quite different from the lives of selfish and benevolent people around them. They take the task of shining seriously and look forward to reflecting God's love for all eternity.

Every day, Everywhere

Strategic Christians search for ways to share and demonstrate light every day. This is what Mark Greene refers to as an integrated life. In his book *Thank God It's Monday*, Greene writes about the call to integrate our faith with our work (job) and all other aspects of our lives.[100] If there is a significant separation between how I shine when I'm with Christian friends and how I live in all other settings, my discipleship is incomplete and inauthentic. A strategic person seeks to shine 24-7 all year long. The strategic are available to God as full-time workers although they may not be commissioned by a church or paid for their service. Our role in changing the world begins but does not end with shining well in our normal daily lives. Here is one example.

I was sitting in a small waiting area connected to a CT room in a radiology office. I was a bit anxious about what the test might discover, but then voices coming from the next room interrupted my thoughts. I recognized the voice of the patient ahead of me. When he had entered the outer lobby an hour earlier, he spoke to everyone in a way that communicated genuine care. He seemed happy to be alive. It was a dark and cold morning, but this guy brought warmth and light into the room. Alone with the CT technician, he now seemed to lift his lantern a bit higher. I overheard muttered communication about the examination, and then the patient rerouted the conversation. It went something like this: "I'm excited about taking this little test. No matter what this machine discovers, I will be fine. God is good. You know he loves us and he's always with us, right? Thank you for helping me today."

This man knows he is blessed to be a blessing, and he lifts high his lantern of God's love. This integrated life and witness is most likely to happen when we begin our days praying for opportunities to shine and we pay attention to the Spirit throughout the day. This is a critical part of a strategic lifestyle.

More than Generous

Strategic Christians think carefully about their stewardship of the resources and blessings entrusted to them by God: time, competencies, possessions, networks, and the ability to pray. This lifestyle involves more than generosity. The strategic seek the highest ROI (return on investment) on the use of their blessings and resources. To achieve a good ROI and reach other goals, we must carefully manage our assets. Todd Massey, US head of investments and advice at J.P. Morgan Private Bank, offers this advice for meeting financial goals: "Have a plan, diversify risk, and have the discipline to remain invested over time."[101] We need a similar commitment to shine brightly. In order to have maximum impact on the world, the strategic develop a plan to utilize their assets and blessings for God's glory. They are intentional and persistent. Strategic Christians share generously and wisely.

Focused for Impact

We all have opportunities to shine and assist others in the journey of life, but some people have larger platforms than others. Imagine that you are charged with strategically using $500 million dollars every year to make the world a better place. That was the job assigned to Darren Walker when he became president of the Ford Foundation in 2013. Soon after assuming leadership, he made a radical change in the approach of the foundation. To have the greatest impact on the world, Walker focused the foundation on one area of need instead of dozens. Walker realized that a focused and deeper engagement was required if their true desire was to change lives and transform communities. The strategic ask questions like Walker's: "What are the systemic reasons that put people out onto the streets?"[102] The strategic prioritize the needs before them and seek to address the underlying causes of problems and pain in order to bring life transformation not just temporary relief.

Courageous

Not unlike those who invest in the stock market, strategic Christians must be aware that there are risks and distracting pressures. This Chinese proverb applies: "The gun will shoot the head of the bird that stands tallest." Cultures and communities encourage us to keep our lights low. I remember being patted on the back by some well-meaning older Christians when I shared passionately about my new faith in Christ. They cautioned, "That's great, but don't get radical." My wife received similar cautions in China when she began to follow Jesus. Every culture provides types of pushbacks to those who would dare to lift high the light of Christ. This resistance is not the general tension between light and darkness, nonbelievers pushing against believers.

I'm referring to the pushback that comes from other people in God's family. The good Jewish people in his hometown did not push back on Jesus because he claimed to be the Messiah. They became indignant about his announcement that God's strategy includes shining grace on Gentiles as well as Jews (Luke 4:24–29). That was too radical for their ethnocentrism. Even when there is pushback, the strategic find ways to demonstrate and share the good news, as "shrewd as snakes and as innocent as doves" (Matthew 10:16).

Points of Light

The approaches of the strategic vary greatly, but here is one example. Pauline Hord (1907–2005) is one of the most strategic people I have ever known. Through all the stages of her life, Pauline was focused on Jesus and the mission of God—even during the years when her physical and financial abilities were declining. As an educator, she had discovered that illiteracy often leads to a life of poverty and crime. As a student of scripture, she learned that prayer is a powerful tool in overcoming darkness. Pauline had a vision of ending illiteracy, poverty, and ignorance of Jesus's grace, and she developed a strategy to achieve her goals by using education and prayer.

I met Pauline when I began serving on the staff of Christ Church Memphis in 1983. I came into the sanctuary at dawn on the day of my first sermon there. I expected the room to be empty, but I saw a woman standing in the balcony. She was praying. I soon learned that Miss Pauline, as many of us addressed her, prayed over every pew before the worship service every Sunday. Years later, I asked Miss Pauline to help me design a prayer room at the church. When I asked what she thought about having a kneeling bench, she smiled and waited a few seconds before replying. "That's a good idea. But most people can only pray on their knees for about ten minutes." I thought to myself, *Yes. Ten minutes would be great*. But Miss Pauline continued, "Chairs will allow us to comfortably pray for hours!" I looked at her glowing face and was reminded that I was in the presence of a humble, loving, powerful saint. Her daily prayer life and her commitment to intercede for others was on a level unknown to me. Although she never used these words, part of her strategy to change the world was intentional, fervent, consistent prayer. Only God knows what miracles were facilitated by the prayers of this dear sister.

Miss Pauline also put feet to her prayers. In 1989, President George H. W. Bush announced that Pauline Hord was one of the recipients of his Points of Light initiative. As he made the presentation in Memphis, President Bush commented, "Somebody at the Mississippi penitentiary at Parchman had been talking about a prisoner there saying he couldn't read a Bible if he had one. So, there's where she stepped forward. And she goes about 100 miles each way to the prison every Wednesday to teach inmates how to read. She's taught nearly 140 of them, and now she's training them to teach others."[103] Miss Pauline was not present to meet the president and receive her award. The ceremony was on a Wednesday, and she spent Wednesdays with her friends at the maximum-security prison. While a crowd of spectators were applauding her in Memphis, Miss Pauline was showing God's love by teaching inmates to read in Mississippi. The applause of heaven she heard that day was far more meaningful than anything that happened in Memphis.

Reflecting on her life, Miss Pauline once told me, "The older you grow, the more you want to know what God wants you to do, to say, to be. Oh, how I want to be the person God wants me to be for his glory. I want to reflect Jesus in the lives that I touch."[104] Pauline Hord closely followed her strategy of changing the world with education and prayer. She found utter joy in serving her Lord. She lifted high the light of Christ as the hope of the world. Her life is an example of strategic living.

The First Driver

People of every age and in any situation can live strategically as they are led and empowered by the Spirit of God. There are at least two motivations, or drivers, for this style of discipleship. One driver is urgency. I have already provided a list of statistics that shows the ominous darkness that engulfs so many. Every day the media and social media highlight suicide, murder, poverty, wars, addiction, depression, racism, human trafficking, hunger, and a thousand other atrocities that illustrate the painful state of our world. The need is urgent. I appreciate the witness of Mamie Till-Mobley, mother of Emmett Till, as she reflected on her son's tragic death: "We are only given a certain amount of time to do what we were sent here to do. You don't have to be around a long time to share the wisdom of a lifetime. You just have to use your time wisely, efficiently. There is no time to waste."[105]

Although the needs are urgent and the days of our lives are numbered, procrastination is common. Perhaps you have heard or said something like "Someone ought to do something about that." I'm weary of hearing of delays in life-changing programs due to well-meaning people being bogged down in bureaucracies and procrastination. I'm weary of benevolent plans that are based on incomplete or outdated information and miss the target of critical need. I feel anger rising in my soul when I learn of yet another example of redundant services while hundreds of millions wait to be served the first time. With so many waiting in darkness, we can do better. Strategic Christians know that every minute counts. They have righteous impatience.

The great strategist Paul directed Titus to encourage his flock to think carefully about the impact of their lives: "Our people must learn to devote themselves to doing what is good, in order to provide for urgent needs and not live unproductive lives" (Titus 3:14). According to Paul's thinking, one characteristic of being a wise and fruitful disciple is the commitment to address urgent needs first. But this way of thinking does not always come naturally. Note that Paul says that Christ followers must "learn" to live and serve in that way. I pray that this book helps you learn in this area. Strategic Christians are driven by a sense of urgency.

The Second Driver

Beyond this passion to respond quickly to critical needs, the strategic are driven by a desire to bring God glory. Revisit Matthew 5:16. Jesus said, "Let your light shine before others, that they may see your good deeds and glorify your Father in heaven." The strategic pray, serve people, show mercy to the broken, and point the way of hope to the lost because they love their neighbors and because when they shine brightly, God receives glory.

I'll discuss this more completely in chapter twelve, but the strategic are motivated by a desire to give God their best. Consider the common dilemma related to acknowledging someone's birthday. I ask myself a series of questions: How well do I know her? Did he give me something for my birthday? What category of gift do I get for her: a text greeting, a phone call, a paper card, a small gift, or a real gift—one that will involve significant effort and money? If I decide that the person is worthy of a real gift, I must determine what he or she might like. No matter what I decide to make or buy, there are different qualities and costs. My bank balance guides me, but not completely. If I really love someone and if he or she is worthy, I will spend whatever it costs to offer a quality gift. Strategic Christians take time, do research, and make the effort to give excellent gifts to Jesus.

In a sense, every day is Jesus's birthday. How we live our lives is our gift to our Savior. What category of gift does he deserve? What type of gift does Jesus desire? Does he yearn for people to know his love? Does he long for broken people to receive kind, healing acts on his behalf? Does he want those actions to happen later or sooner? Does Jesus find joy in temporary solutions to suffering when lasting solutions are available? Strategic Christians are excited about bringing God glory by urgently addressing needs and serving with excellence.

Zeal and Knowledge

People get excited for a variety of reasons. Sometimes our excitement prods us to take appropriate and necessary action. But sometimes our zeal leads us down other paths. The pre-Christian Saul was zealous for his religion and thought he was serving God by persecuting the disciples of Jesus. Proverbs 19:2 cautions that zeal without knowledge can cause more damage than good. In Mark 1:43–45, a man is so excited about being healed from leprosy that he ignores Jesus's command to tell no one. "Instead he went out and began to talk freely, spreading the news.

As a result, Jesus could no longer enter a town openly but stayed outside in lonely places." Zeal without knowledge is not good.

Paul cautions Christ followers to make decisions and plans based on knowledge, not just emotion. "Brothers and sisters, my heart's desire and prayer to God for the Israelites is that they may be saved. For I can testify about them that they are zealous for God, but their zeal is not based on knowledge" (Romans 10:1–2). Well-meaning Christians have often been driven by misinformed zeal. Religious zeal drove Western missionaries to encourage converts in Africa to wear European clothes. Zeal for righteousness has made Christians speak in hateful ways to people with values and lifestyles different from theirs. Benevolent Christians continue to rush into crises and offer types of aid that are not wanted or needed by the residents. Zeal is a two-edged sword. It can create wonderful and loving victories for God's kingdom, but when zeal is uninformed, it can cause hurt, confusion, and loss of respect.

One example of emotional but unwise action is related to the phrase "Hey! Watch this!" It is usually followed by a crash and damage to person and property. The overconfident actor is often a young male trying to impress his peers, but zealots of all ages have fallen into this error. One of my many such moments took place when I was a teenager. As my girlfriend Becky and I exited a movie theater late one night in downtown Jackson, Mississippi, several police cars raced by with sirens blaring. I responded zealously, "Let's follow them." We quickly pulled out, and the chase was on. Right, then left, then another left, and then— oops! I had pulled into the middle of a riot. The large crowd was angry, and we were uninvited intruders. Surrounded by the mob, we couldn't go forward or backward. Becky screamed—or that might have been me. A police officer quickly came to the rescue and parted the crowd so we could leave. Blindly following police cars had seemed like a good idea at time. Perhaps you remember a time in your life when zeal without knowledge led to regrettable action.

The strategic are aware that needs are urgent, but they don't jump without thinking. They listen to the call of the Spirit, but they also take time to do research and develop plans that are both biblical and helpful in meeting the ministry goals. Our initial response to a need tends to be emotional and may produce action that hurts more than it helps. Different needs demand different types of responses. A strategy for assisting someone who collapses and doesn't have a pulse might include an emotional attempt to provide CPR. In this case, we are told to not hesitate because you can't hurt a dead person. Our response to someone drowning in a rushing river requires a different approach. Without a wise plan, both the would-be rescuer and the victim flailing in the river may die. Sometimes helping hurts. I highly recommend the writings of Steve Corbett and Brian Fikkert, and Marvin Olasky. Their writings provide guidance on how to create ministry strategies that truly help people.[106] The zeal and emotions of the strategic are tempered with knowledge and planning. It is quite amazing what God can do through a life that has both zeal and knowledge.

Think

The Spirit helps the strategic develop a sense of adventure about the needs of the world and our role in God's mission. The strategic think big. Many people can feed a hungry family, but it takes a different kind of commitment and thinking to end hunger and prevent diseases. Alan Turing told his team of scientists and mathematicians that they would win World War II by breaking the Enigma Code used by the Nazi's. They broke the code, and it is estimated that their work shortened the war by two years and saved 14 million lives.[107] Strategic Christians consider ways to impact as many lives as possible.

The strategic also take time to think through the details of achieving big goals. Exhaustive research, careful planning, and courageous decision-making play key roles in military campaigns, successful businesses, great music, beautiful art, and moving worship services. In the parable of the shrewd manager (Luke 16:1–15), the dishonest man is commended because he acted shrewdly. Although his ethics were lopsided, he took time to think and develop a plan. "For the people of this world are more shrewd in dealing with their own kind than are the people of the light" (8). Jesus is making a statement about the people of light and the importance of being intentional about how we use our time, blessings, and opportunities. William MacAskill comments that "being unreflective often means being ineffective."[108] Successful projects are not thrown together with the hope that the combining of several good components will produce a good outcome. This approach may work well when I'm making vegetable soup but prove disastrous for other projects. Each act of worship, musical note, business tactic, and football play is chosen because it uniquely moves toward the goal of the designer. Although we continue to be surrounded by countless opportunities to be benevolent, the strategic think carefully about how they can best shine for Jesus.

Utilitarianism and Effective Altruism

Although I knew little about the history of altruism and utilitarianism before I began research for this manuscript, I was certain that I was not the first to seek more effective ways of meeting the needs of people. In the seventeenth century, an ethical theory began to emerge that became known as utilitarianism. It generally holds that the most ethical choice is the one that will produce the greatest good for the greatest number of people. In the twentieth century, a movement began that merged the concerns of utilitarianism with the passion of altruists. Effective altruism (EA) is defined as "a philosophy and social movement focused on answering one question: How can we best help others?"[109] The effective altruism movement has roots in academic philosophy, but in the past two decades, thought and business leaders like Peter Singer, William MacAskill, Elon Musk, and Melinda and Bill Gates have followed and advocated the values of the movement.[110]

There is overlap between Jesus's invitation to live strategically and the priorities of these altruists. Christians may have the same desire to meet needs in profound and effective ways[111], but our ministry is inherently different from the approaches of EA activists and utilitarianists of other faiths or no faith. Although the action involved in meeting a need may look identical—such as feeding hungry children—strategic Christians are driven by three realities:

- Each person is created in the image of God and is so valuable that Christ died for him or her.
- In addition to tangible needs, each person has spiritual and relational needs that cannot be satisfied by anything or anyone other than our Creator.
- When we serve others, we demonstrate our love for God and bring glory to God.

The Spirit First and Always

A word of caution. We have the tendency to think we are in control. Strategic planning without listening to the Spirit may result in plans that are out of sync with God's priorities, and any results will be limited by mere human intelligence and strength. On the other hand, the ministry efforts of praying Christians may sometimes appear overly zealous and unplanned, but God may use the ministry to do amazing things. At first glance, the ministry of Philip in Acts 8 may seem strange and nonstrategic. Called by the Spirit, Philip left a successful ministry in Samaria to go stand on a road in the desert. This ministry strategy led to the conversion of only one person. This new believer, however, is thought to have helped birth the church in Ethiopia. Only later would Philip's obedience be understood as a strategic move that resulted in thousands of conversions on a different continent. In some situations, there is no time to do research and careful planning. Sometimes we just pray and obey the Spirit's guidance. Strategic Christians pray and listen to the Spirit before they move out, as they serve, and as they finish. We are never in control of anything except our own lives and our prayers.

The Church runs with Jesus in his mission to love and transform lost and hurting people (Mt 4:18–19). The concept of running implies intentionality, sacrifice, and a specific goal. Strategic living is an urgent response to the most pressing needs of the world. Strategic living requires an intimate knowledge of the King and his values. It is fueled by the desire for God to receive glory. It is guided by our desire to give God excellent and appropriate gifts. Our salvation does not depend on us living strategically. It is, rather, a choice related to our love for our Savior and our desire to please him. Peter encouraged church leaders to serve faithfully by appealing to this same desire: "Not because you have to, but because you want to please God" (1 Peter 5:2 MSG).

Summary

The strategic shine brightly because they allow God to transform their attitudes toward light and darkness. As you seek God's help in reclaiming your identity as the light of the world, the Spirit will change how you see your role in God's mission and the way you live out your faith. In this transformation, passion will replace curiosity, urgency will replace idleness, expectancy will replace a lack of faith, engagement will replace spectatorship, intentionality will replace haphazardness, and daily shining will replace episodic shining. A casual understanding of shining for God will be replaced by a spirit of adventure that seeks to change the world and present Jesus with an excellent gift. Strategic Christians listen to the Spirit's guidance and shine in ways that are in keeping with God's nature. They strive to

1. proclaim the good news of Jesus Christ and demonstrate God's grace in response to the diverse needs of people;
2. address the needs of people culturally near as well as those of people who have a language, race, religion, economic status, or zip code different than theirs;
3. address the underlying causes of problems and pain in order to bring life transformation instead of temporary relief; and
4. bring glory to our loving, holy, gracious, eternal, and amazing Creator God.

Strategic living flows from an intentionality to be the best possible steward of God's blessings in order that the maximum number of people join God's family, are transformed by grace, and God is honored. Once we taste this type of lifestyle, we can never be satisfied with less. Selfish, benevolent, or strategic—none of these lifestyles are totally foreign to any of us. You may have visited all of these in a frustrating cycle, but which one best describes your approach to life and ministry today? Most importantly, which style do you want to define and dominate your response to God's blessings?

The following chapters will provide steps and guidelines to help you shine more brightly than you have ever imagined. Each of us is on a journey to understand and better fulfill our calling to be the light of the world.

Be the Change

CHAPTER 9: STRATEGIC LIGHT

Consider

> ➤ Strategic living flows from an intentionality to be the best possible steward of God's blessings in order that the maximum number of lives are transformed and God is honored. Which part of this definition is most significant for you?
> ➤ How does this concept make you feel about God's mission and your role in it?

Interact

> ➤ Talk about the ways Miss Pauline fits the definition of the strategic. Do you see the two motivations in her life: an urgent approach to needs and a desire to see God glorified with excellence?
> ➤ To what degree do these motivations influence the way you shine?

Pray

> ▸ Thank God for the miraculous and mysterious gift of prayer.
> ▸ Ask God to bless and transform those who are incarcerated, those who minister with them, and those who have suffered because of the decisions of those in prison.

Act

> ▸ What is your chief motivation? Finish this sentence: "I want to shine more strategically because…."
> ▸ Call or visit a person or group that you feel meets the definition of the Strategic.

HIGHER LIGHT

CHAPTER 10

Our Light Journeys

He said to them, "Do you bring in a lamp to put it under a bowl
or a bed? Instead, don't you put it on its stand?"

—Mark 4:21

Highlights

> The Christian life is a journey. As we grow in grace, we can
  expect our shining to also grow.
> Our journey to lift our lanterns higher involves various
  influences, seasons, mistakes, and victories.
> The terms "selfish," "benevolent," and "strategic" refer to
  decisions we make or philosophies we hold regarding how we
  use our blessings to impact the world for Christ.

What graduations have you had? I was present to receive my diploma
when I graduated from Wingfield High School. I skipped the ceremony
at Mississippi State University, but I walked the aisle to humbly received
the master of divinity diploma at Asbury Theological Seminary four
years later. These pieces of paper called diplomas certify that I satisfied
the basic requirements of an institution. These degrees do not mean I
am smart or a master of divinity. Graduations should be appreciated as

stepping-stones. Graduations mean we are a bit more ready to serve than we would have been otherwise. Graduations position us to learn even more in the future. A graduation is equally a beginning and an ending.

The Christian life, our experience as the light of the world, is a journey that involves various influences, seasons, mistakes, and victories. The Apostle Peter's journey involved at least two conversions. He was converted to Christ, and we see him faithfully serving other Jewish converts in Jerusalem (Acts 2). Later, the focus of Peter's ministry was converted. He moved beyond a ministry focused on his own culture but blind to the rest of the world (Acts 10). Although Scripture refers to him as the apostle to the Jews, Peter finally saw the beauty and importance of all people (nations, cultures, language groups, castes, and ethnicities) as he grasped the global and ethnic ramifications of Jesus's commissioning (Matthew 28:19 and Acts 1:8). The impact of Peter and the other disciples continued to increase as their faith grew and they followed the Spirit. There's no reason that we shouldn't expect to have a similar journey of increasing light and impact.

Loving Jesus and My Close Neighbors

Not unlike Peter's experience, my journey of faith has involved a series of conversions, decisions, or graduations. Some of my attitudes and behaviors changed quickly, but the transformation of others took decades. At age seventeen, I was converted by God's grace through faith in Jesus as I turned from darkness to light. I graduated from a life of almost total selfishness to a life desiring to honor God. Jesus used people like our youth minister Sam Morris to lead me into God's forever family and help me begin living as a cruciform disciple. My newly converted friends and I passionately responded to Christ's call to love him and share his love with others. We prayed with friends in the hallways at school. We started prayer groups before class and passed out Christian literature. I often wrote Bible verses on the mirror in the employee restroom at the grocery store where I worked after school. I shared the good news wherever I decided to go each day, but my witness was haphazard and my light didn't shine very far. Lost and hurting people beyond my routine and culture almost never entered my mind. I was hanging out in Jerusalem and practically ignoring Judea, Samaria, and the uttermost parts of the earth (Acts 1:8). I was passionate about impacting people with God's love, but I used my personal experiences to make global assumptions. Because I saw God changing lives around me, I had an optimistic though naive sense about the overall transformation of the world. I didn't know what I didn't know. Unconsciously, I also assumed that my witness would be limited to people like me: people in the southern part of the United States who were English speakers, white, educated, and middle-class. And it was. I underestimated what it means to be the light of the world.

Three Streams Converge

I continued with this passionate but limited style of Christian witness until three streams converged to propel me to graduation number two. In 1983, I joined the staff of Christ Church Memphis, pastored by Maxie Dunnam. Maxie was the first world Christian I ever met. His eyes, heart, interpretation of scripture, and prayers went far beyond my little world. Maxie introduced me to dynamic Christ followers in many countries, and I heard about levels of need that blew my mind. For the first time, my prayer routines began to include people in cultures and lands far from Tennessee. My eyes were opening.

The second stream that merged with this new global vision came out of my experience in youth ministry. Like many youth ministries, the program I led included Sunday-morning classes, Sunday-night activities, Bible studies, retreats, fun trips, and mission projects. After ten years of youth ministry in three states, I took time to do a progress report on my ministry. I was shocked by one revelation. The youth who were most involved in missions and service opportunities were the ones who were most consistent in their faith, dependable, kind, willing to volunteer, passionate about Bible study, and free from the common behavioral challenges that trip up many teenagers. It seemed that God was doing deeper and more lasting work in the lives of those who followed Jesus in service beyond their own networks and cultures. I began to explore what this meant for the way I minister and how this revelation might be related to scripture and my calling.

The third stream involved a farewell to youth ministry when the church leaders and I decided God was calling me to head up the church's outreach ministries. In my work with teenagers, I had participated in rural and urban ministries with disadvantaged people in the United States, but my understanding of the greater world was limited. As we grew the outreach ministry of the church, however, I began to lead short-term mission teams to places like El Salvador, Costa Rica, Brazil, Morocco, Russia, and China. This gave me opportunities to listen to and learn from brothers and sisters in cultures far different from mine. The world and God's kingdom were much larger than I had imagined.

These three streams combined into a roaring river that forced me to think and pray deeply about my blessings, my experiences, and my growing understanding of the complex needs in the world. Eventually, I began to realize that the Spirit was opening my eyes to my potential and my calling: I could be involved in God's mission far beyond my culture and imagination. Like John Wesley, I began to see that the world was my parish. I was already serving as a missions pastor, but this fresh calling was not about an organizational title. God was inviting me to adjust my worldview, the ways I prayed and served, and my expectations about how God might use me. With a mixture of faith and anxiety, I prayed, "Lord, use me in your global mission any way you choose." I count this as my second big decision, conversion, and graduation in my journey of light. I heard God's invitation and I took a step of faith. I was excited, but soon I was confused and a bit frightened. What would it look like for me to be the light of the world and shine beyond my region of the US? What might this cost me? For a season, I continued living and serving in ways much like I had been, but I knew God was not finished with me. I kept praying, and I began to look for people who might understand my questions and longings.

God's Word

The third graduation in my journey to shine more brightly also involved many steps. Somewhere along the way, I began to create a list of Bible references that relate to what I eventually called strategic living. This list gets longer every day.[112] I still wonder how I could have missed this clear theme in scripture for so long. One of my favorite Bible stories about strategic living is found in Mark 2:1-5. I love the persistence and creativity of the men who lowered their paralyzed friend through a roof in order for Jesus to heal him. The foundational passage for strategic living, however, is Matthew 5:14–16, where Jesus identifies his followers as the light of the world and invites us to make the effort to lift our lanterns high. In a sense, this passage can be seen as an overarching theme for the three chapters in Matthew that are called the Sermon on the Mount. The discourse describes the lifestyle of one who seeks to shine brightly for God's glory. It encourages us to think carefully about how our actions impact others and influence how people think about God. What does it mean to be merciful and make peace, to love our enemies, to give to the needy, and to pray for God's kingdom to come? What does Jesus mean when he says that he didn't come for the healthy, but for the sick? My survey of the Bible revealed that faithful Christ followers will live cruciform lives and be intentional about impacting lost and hurting people near and far for the glory of God.[113]

Frustration

Step-by-step God was changing my life. At one point in my journey, I reflected on statistics like those I shared in chapter six and noticed the significant gap between the calling of the Church and the billions of hurting and lost people who were unreached by the gospel and untouched by Christian compassion. There were many ministry accomplishments to celebrate, but I became convicted that a status quo attitude toward the remaining task was unfaithful. With my head swimming in frustration, I asked myself, "Why keep a lamp under a bowl when there is so much darkness screaming for light?" I didn't want to be a poor steward of God's blessings in the face of so much need. At that point, the Holy Spirit made all the disappointing ministry statistics very personal to me. I realized that every December I celebrate Christmas by thanking God for loving the world so much that he gave his only Son. And yet billions of people have not learned that there is something to celebrate. I drink as much clean water as I want every day. And yet over 2 billion people walk miles to find relatively clean water or drink water I wouldn't offer my dog. My understanding of the needs of the world had changed earlier, but now I began to realize that something about my approach to God's mission needed to change. The Spirit began adding excitement and hope to my frustration.

Focus for Impact

In my role as a missions leader, I discovered the writings of Bob Lupton and John Perkins.[114] Their urban ministry strategies involve changing a city one neighborhood at a time by setting ministry target areas and then mobilizing partnerships and resources to impact all aspects of that community. At that point, my personal ministry and my missions leadership had been passionate but unfocused. We poured time, prayer, and money into various projects without any real metrics or boundaries. These investments made us feel better, but the lives of the intended ministry recipients were often unchanged. In the spirit of Lupton and Perkins, I adjusted the way I approached ministry. Eventually Christ Church began to focus on one community in Memphis, the Binghampton neighborhood. Our intentionality slowly began to produce tangible results: improved housing, better health-care options, lower crime, and enhanced community pride. More progress has been made over the decades—spiritual and temporal—because one church developed a long-term strategy that focused resources and prayer on a specific neighborhood. I learned that a church, family, or person who desires to have maximum impact must consider ways to focus.

Research as Well as Prayer

It didn't take long for me to realize that it is difficult to know where to focus. We pray for discernment, but our tendency is to favor areas where we have experience or personal contacts. This subjective approach often results in a focus that is not on areas with the highest needs and fewest points of light. Research is not a substitute for prayer: they go hand in hand. The writings and lectures of Ray Bakke, founder of International Urban Associates, alerted me to the importance of research in determining where to focus.[115] Thorough research provides objective information about the most urgent areas of need, and additional research reveals the best methods to address needs in the areas of focus. There are no shortcuts to research. Heed the caution of Ester Duflo. Without research, our tactics will make as much sense as fighting "illness by applying leeches."[116]

Measure What You Can

One day I asked myself the question many others have considered regarding ministry: How can I know whether my ministry efforts are successful? How can I know what impact my light is making? It became increasingly important for me to find a way to know which tactics are most effective in achieving the goals that are valued by God. This was the beginning of my search to understand the relationship between ministry and metrics. Once I saw the importance of metrics, I realized that many things are relatively easy to measure: meals served, baptisms, and homes repaired. It is, however, far more difficult for mere mortals to measure how God is moving in another's soul, but we can do our best to quantify what we can as Barnabas did in Acts 11. The use of metrics better positions us to have appropriate gratitude and to learn how to have greater impact. Among other disappointments, the failure to use metrics can lead to people championing a program although its effectiveness has been declining for years. The refusal to use metrics is a decision to keep light under a basket.

Say No to Say Yes

After serving in various ministry roles in churches, a seminary, and a nonprofit mission, I was invited by Glenn Gutek to join the staff of Awake

Consulting and Coaching. He introduced me to a book and concept that would provide significant guidance for me: *Necessary Endings* by Henry Cloud. As he introduces the universal need to create endings, Cloud makes this statement: "Getting to the next level always requires ending something, leaving it behind, and moving on."[117] Successful students, athletes, entrepreneurs, and people trying to change the world create endings so they can move closer to their ultimate goals. To shine as brightly as we can, we must cancel or radically change tactics and programs that do not produce the desired results according to our goals and metrics. The Spirit was helping me realize that I needed to begin saying no to some good and benevolent opportunities so that I could say yes to some strategic opportunities to spread the good news and bring God glory. Even Jesus said no. "The people were looking for him and when they came to where he was, they tried to keep him from leaving them. But he said, 'I must proclaim the good news of the kingdom of God to the other towns also, because that is why I was sent'" (Luke 4:42–43).

Putting It All Together

The Christian life is a journey. As we grow in grace, we can expect our shining to also grow. I have much more to learn, but the Spirit has elevated my understanding of what it means for me to be the light of the world. God revealed the difference between unintentionally hiding my lantern under my bed and lifting high the lamp of God's grace. Step-by-step, God moved me away from selfishness and a style of shining that was haphazardly benevolent. The Spirit changed my attitude about shining, and I began to change the ways I participated in God's mission. I learned to appreciate the importance of focus, research, metrics, and the necessity of sometimes saying no in order to shine brightly. After walking with Jesus for over twenty years, I finally put it all together and made a commitment to live the rest of my life in the land of the strategic. This long series of revelations I received and decisions I made led me to graduation number three.

My use of the concept of graduation should not imply that the terms "selfish," "benevolent," and "strategic" are the names of phases in the Christian life. Fundamentally, these are decisions we make or philosophies we hold—consciously or not—regarding how we will use our blessings to impact the world for Christ. We may visit the three styles of shining multiple times in our journeys. We tend, however, to allow one style to dominate our shining. But hear this important reminder: God loves you no more or less at any point in your journey. God's love is not tied to how brightly we shine. God loves us because that is who God is.

My journey to shining more brightly has been long but wonderful. It has not been a nice linear Miami-to-Orlando-to-Atlanta route. I wandered around a bit. I learned, unlearned, and relearned lessons along the way. Even today I do not to live full-time in the zip code of strategic shining. I regress into selfishness and benevolence too often, but my goal is fixed: maximum impact for God's glory.

I have introduced you to some of the key chapters in my journey to understand and better fulfill my calling to be the light of the world. My journey may be similar to or quite different from yours. Don't let the fact that I am in vocational ministry distract you from the reality that all God's children wrestle with these same questions, struggles, and godly yearnings. Be encouraged. If Jesus can make these changes in my life, he can transform anyone. I have been a slow learner; you can do better. When I began my journey to shine more brightly, I often felt alone and had no idea where I was heading. Gracious friends, the school of hard knocks, and the Holy Spirit were my teachers. In this book, I am sharing the lessons I have learned as a way to help others who seek to shine more brightly.

The first phase in reclaiming your identity as the light of the world is the process of allowing the Spirit to transform your attitude toward the needs of the world and your role in God's light mission. All the previous chapters have highlighted this transformation. The next chapter provides guidance in how to create an approach to shining that is aligned with your transformed attitude toward shining.

Be the Change

CHAPTER 10: OUR LIGHT JOURNEYS

Consider

> ‣ Think about the last graduation ceremony you attended. Recall your emotions and thoughts that day.
> ‣ Is there a nonacademic graduation you need to be working on in order to help you shine more brightly?

Interact

> ‣ Share how your journey of light is similar to and different from the author's.

Pray

> ‣ Thank God for graciously accepting you just the way you are.
> ‣ Ask God to help you be discerning and courageous as you seek to shine brighter for the cause of Christ.
> ‣ Pray for those who are translating scripture for language groups that do not have the Bible in their own language.

Act

> ‣ List some priorities, opportunities, or habits that you want to say no to in order to say yes to living more strategically.

CHAPTER 11

Building a Taller Lampstand

> Suppose one of you wants to build a tower. Will he not first sit down and estimate the cost to see if he has enough money to complete it?
>
> —Luke 14:28

Highlights

> - Here is an eight-step process to build a taller lampstand and begin living more strategically.
> - If this template is not a good fit, create your own; but changing the way you shine will take significant time, prayer, research, thinking, and discussion.
> - The ways we live strategically may change in the various stages of life, but there are defining characteristics of lives that seek to have maximum impact on the world.

In a letter to her husband John Adams in 1774, Abigail Adams pushed him to move beyond good intentions and do more than applaud others as they worked to achieve independence for the American colonies. "You cannot be, I know, nor do I wish to see you, an inactive spectator … We have too many high-sounding words, and too few actions that correspond with them."[118] I pray that the previous chapters have helped you better understand our calling to shine brightly and the purpose of serving God in this way. This chapter will shift from "high-sounding words" to action. Instead of just talking about how the world and the Church need to change, let's focus on what it means to *be the change*. How can your orthodoxy produce faithful orthopraxy? How can your transformed attitude about being the light of the world be demonstrated in your life?

Living strategically takes more than hoping and praying. It requires more than haphazard shining as we go about our daily tasks. It takes intentionality and hard work. The Apostle Paul had a clear vision for the impact of his life: "To win as many as possible" (1 Corinthians 9:19). His plan was to proclaim and demonstrate freedom in Christ in such a way that the maximum number of Gentiles and Jews might be transformed by grace. He was focused and self-disciplined about his mission of light. "I do not run like someone running aimlessly" (26). In order to honor Christ and have maximum impact on the world, he accepted the hard work and pain that are always part of achieving a high goal. Paul prepared to win.

We can shine strategically in a myriad of ways each day, but creating a plan to shine is a tactic to efficiently connect your attitude about shining with the other realities in your life. I call this "building a taller lampstand." Your lampstand is the system of shining that thoughtfully relates your blessings to the needs of the world and God's calling. Faithful participation in God's global mission of light involves a commitment to use our blessings so that the maximum number of lives are transformed and God is glorified.

Until we allow the Spirit to develop an attitude of adventure in us, most people will have little desire to create a system of shining although the world is big, the needs are overwhelming, and our calling is urgent. Some people, however, are born with a pioneering spirit. When I was four, my mother convinced my father to build a fence around our small back yard. She desperately needed a secured place to send me so I could burn off energy during the day. Just as my dad was finishing the last section, my mom looked up and saw me scaling the new fence on the way to my friend's house. When she shared this old memory with me, she smiled and added, "You always had places to go." My disposition has always included a desire for adventure and a curiosity about the road less traveled. I realize that you may have a different disposition.

This difference need not impede your desire to build a taller lampstand. Ask God to stretch your capacity for adventure. You may also be led to partner with someone who has more of a pioneering attitude. Being adventurous does not necessarily include long trips. It does mean that you are concerned about needs far beyond your comfort zone, and you are open to shining anywhere God leads you.

By nature, I am also a planner. I even create detailed spreadsheets for the vacation trips we take. These traits have served me well as I create shining systems and a taller lampstand. You may love the details and process I am recommending, but the steps may seem too linear, too difficult, or too boring for some people. How you approach this process will be greatly influenced by your personality, but hear this caution: God's calling and your desire to shine brightly are too important to let a personality trait derail your journey of light. By following a process like this, you can shine the light of Jesus brighter and further than you have imagined. If you are not ready to take the steps I recommend, that is okay. Scan them quickly, and then read the remaining chapters. You can return to this section later. If my template is not a good fit for you, create your own plan to shine more brightly.

As you consider building a taller lampstand, you should begin to feel a bit of excitement. God wants to use you to bless and transform the world. Light from your lamp may eventually make a difference in the lives of women enduring the horror of human trafficking in your state, hungry children in Bangladesh, the unchurched in your neighborhood, or the spiritually lost in a "creative access" country like North Korea. The types of needs, the locations of the needs, and the methods you choose to address the needs will flow out of the building process below. When we establish priorities, create plans, and pray fervently, we join the transforming work God is already doing, and miracles happen.

Preparing to Build

A good builder takes time to adequately prepare before the first hole is dug or the first brick is laid. Before you launch into the process of building a taller lampstand, prepare by addressing these five concerns.

Take time to remember who God is and who you are. First, think deeply about of God. Read several Bible passages that illustrate the character of the Father, Son, and Holy Spirit. Second, consider the power and abundance of darkness in the world, and recall some ways you have seen God's light overcome darkness. Third, remember that you are God's child and his Spirit lives in you. You are the light of the world. God is already using you as a change agent, but the Spirit is calling you to lift your lantern higher. Throughout the centuries, God has given direction and power to courageous women, men, and children who dared to pray, "Lord, use me to change the world for your glory." Pray those words now.

Prepare to share the reason for the hope within you. There are two basic tools every believer needs to shine brightly: a testimony and a way to guide someone who wants to join God's family. According to 1 Peter 3:15, we need a kind and clear way to answer questions like "Why are you a Christian, and how did that happen?"[119] We also need a short and biblically accurate way to answer the question "How can I become a member of God's family?" Regardless of what needs or strategies you choose, these two tools will help you lift Christ's light high. Preparing these will take some time. As you work on these tools, continue with the following steps.

Identify the core motivations for your desire to shine brightly. Why are you creating a plan to guide your generosity and your impact on the world? If this is a family project, each member can write down his or her own thoughts. Share, discuss, and consolidate the ideas into a motivation statement that might be something like "We want our lives, prayers and possessions to have maximum impact on the world for God's glory," or perhaps "I want to live in a way that changes the world and makes Jesus smile."

Get in touch with the way you make decisions regarding God's will and your involvement in God's mission. Many people make philanthropy and altruism decisions based on feelings and solicitation. People are emotionally moved by a particular need, or they respond to a personal invitation. To begin living more strategically, something must change in the way we make decisions about God's mission. Make a commitment to not be unduly swayed by subjectivity or the winsome appeal of a person or group. The strategic make light decisions based on two things: accurate information on needs and the direction of the Spirit over a period of days or weeks.

Lastly, think of the ways you have used your time, prayers, and other resources to demonstrate and communicate God's love in the past. Be as specific as you can. Make a list of activities, donations, prayers, and other ways that you have intentionally reached out in love to bless others. The list may be short or long, but celebrate what God has done through you. God has already used you as the light of the world, but the best is yet to come.

Building a Taller Lampstand

It's time to start building. If a spouse or other family members will be part of the process, gather everyone together. Read through the entire process and then begin working on the steps. Make notes as you move through each step. Be patient but diligent. You are reclaiming your identity as the light of the world.

1. Take Inventory

Make a list of your assets, resources, and blessings. Consider things like your time, talents, relationships, possessions, finances, and education. Write everything down. Your ability to pray is a foundational blessing. Don't forget to consider your own brokenness. Many of us have resources to offer those walking in darkness that flow out of the pain of our own mistakes and histories. Each person and family has a unique set of circumstances and gifts. Review your long and detailed list. You are blessed. Some, or perhaps all, of these will become part of your strategy to shine more brightly.

2. Define Terms

The meanings of words like "outreach" and "missions" have become cloudy. Clarity is important for the success of any endeavor. Builders must agree on the architect's goal and the definition of key terms, such as "inch" and "level." Review what scripture says about charity, good works, evangelism, missions, outreach, and service. Now create the definition you will use for "shining." You might also want to reread the part of chapter six that deals with definitions. Your definition will be different from your neighbor's or your church's, and that is okay.

3. Research Needs

Get information from the internet, church and mission leaders, and other sources, and then create a list of twenty pressing but underserved needs: ten in your community and ten beyond your community. This will take some time. You may have begun reading this chapter with an assumption that you know the type of needs you want to address. Maybe that is where you will end up, but stay open. God may use you in other ways and places. There are wonderful exceptions, but normally we feel called to act after we are made aware of a need. In order to know where and how to shine brightly, you need to do your homework regarding needs.

4. Establish Values

Look over the list of underserved needs you created. Which of those have the strongest connection with your history, assets, resources, and inner passion? What needs push your buttons and seem the most urgent? Out of the twenty needs you listed in step three, which five do you value most? A family might come up with a list of needs to address or demographic groups to serve like this: the education of children, the homeless, people with cancer, victims of crime, and communities that don't have a Bible in their language. Refuse to ignore certain needs because they seem to be beyond your capacity to address. Trust the process and the Spirit. Decisions about locations, partners, resources, and specific tactics come later.

5. Listen Carefully

There is a difference between asking God to bless your plans and inviting God to lead you. Remember that the moon shines only as it basks in the light of the sun. Meditate on Colossians 4:2–5 and take a week or more to listen to God. Hold up to God the list of needs you selected in step four, and ask, "What are you calling us to pursue now?" Thank God for the miracle of prayer and the guidance of the Holy Spirit.

6. Focus for Impact

In archery and in project planning, coaches advise us to "aim small, miss small." You will not be able to pursue all the needs that concern you—at least not at the same time. Review the five needs you selected and prayed about in steps four and five. Now highlight the one or two needs that God seems to be asking you to initially address. You may change areas of focus later, but this is a starting point. This step requires saying no to some good programs and deep needs in order to say yes to options that you feel more called to pursue. Without focusing, it will be difficult to build partnerships or establish metrics. You will be busy, but you may have little to show for your labor and generosity. As you focus on the two needs God is calling you to address, begin to consider what aspects of your history, assets, and other resources might be used by God to address those needs.

7. Build Relationships

Few good and lasting accomplishments are achieved without respectful and mutually beneficial relationships. The Apostle Paul had much to offer to the young church in Rome, but notice his humility and mutuality: "I long to see you so that I may impart to you some spiritual gift to make you strong – that is, that you and I may be mutually encouraged by each other's faith" (Romans 1:11–12). As you begin to implement your plans, you will want to begin meaningful relationships with two groups of people: the people you hope to serve and people who are already serving these types of needs. First, do research to understand more about the people you hope to serve. If possible, spend time with them or people like them before you finalize plans to address needs. Listen to their dreams. Second, find out what ministries or people are already addressing the types of needs you want to address. Explore their strategies and ways you might be involved. Your light partner might be an organization, your church, or a neighbor who also sees the need and wants to intervene. Our light mission is too big and too important to go alone. As many have said, "It takes the whole church to bring the whole gospel to the whole world."[120]

8. Establish Strategy

This step answers one big question: How will you address the needs you have prioritized? In step three, you used research to create a list of underserved needs. You now need good research to help you explore strategies to address those needs. Finally, review your notes from the previous steps and write up a plan to address the needs you selected. Stay flexible. Watch for changes in the needs, a drop in the effectiveness of your approach, and redirection by the Spirit. No matter how much planning you do, things will happen that you did not anticipate. You may follow a strategy that is similar to the approach of another family or group. You may, however, need to innovate. A good strategy will answer these questions:

> Goal: What specific needs are you addressing, and what do you hope happens?
> Timing: What are the target dates for your first action steps? How will you know when it is time to change or stop your participation in this strategy?
> Prayer: Who will be your prayer partners and how will they know specific ways to pray for the ministry?
> Resources: What resources (time, talents, possessions, contacts, prayer) will you use to execute the strategy? How can everyone in

the family or team be involved? How will this support fit in with the ways you are supporting your church and other ministries?

› Partners: If you are working with ministry partners (your church, other individuals, or organizations), how will that work? What are their responsibilities and yours?

› Roles: Who in your family or team has primary responsibility for the various parts of the strategy?

› Metrics: As you consider strategies to address the needs of these people, you are envisioning a different and brighter future for them. How will you know if your ministry is successful? Some important types of progress are difficult to measure. Be diligent to measure and track what you can.

› Coaching: Do you need help in creating or editing your strategy? Find a mission leader or more experienced friend to guide you.[121]

Review and Celebrate

Guided by your goals and metrics, review your ministry strategy at least annually. If you don't make the effort to evaluate the ministry, your analysis and decision-making will likely be subjective and emotional. The appropriate use of metrics, however, brings objectivity and clarity for celebrations as well as course corrections that need to be made. Throughout the year, the strategic take time to learn and relearn, think and rethink—but especially at yearend. An annual review will answer questions like the following:

› What do the metrics suggest about the effectiveness of your effort to impact these specific needs?

› What worked? What didn't?

› Where and how did you sense God's presence, power, and joy in the ministry?

› What did you learn about the people you hoped to serve?

› How well did you execute your role in the partnership?

› Will you continue to address these same needs? If so, will you continue the same strategy or use a different approach?

Regardless of how successful you feel your efforts have been, make time to celebrate all that God has done through you or in spite of you. The celebration can be elaborate or simple. It could involve just your family or all the key people. Be creative. Plan a special meal, go to a well-liked restaurant, or meet in a place that has special meaning for you or your strategy (such as an ethnic restaurant related to the people you serve). You might host a video conference with key people if a physical gathering is impractical.

I'll never forget my participation in such a celebration in North Africa. A lavish party was thrown to celebrate the completion of a two-year project that brought fresh water to ten Muslim villages by tapping into a spring at the top of a nearby mountain. One part of the plan—unknown to most of the partners—addressed the spiritual needs of the area. A civil engineer (sponsored by Partners International) went to every home in the area to interview the people and explain the project. This gave him opportunities to share the good news as trusting relationships developed and God opened doors.

On the day of the celebration, representatives from each of the partner groups met in the amazing home of a village leader. Government officials, village leaders, and the staff of Partners International were present.[122] My friend Tom and I were there to represent what was known as the American partners (our church). Fifty local people and four foreign visitors sat on beautiful wool rugs at low tables. The climax of the meal was the serving of a roasted ram—head, horns, legs, and all. With great fanfare, it was served on a platter carried in by four men. The meal was so big that the last course was a creamy white paste that was translated into English as "antacid."

As was their custom at the opening of new businesses or homes, a guest was asked to sing a blessing. All eyes turned to me. I panicked but quickly searched my internal database for songs about water. The only song that came to mind was an old chorus, and I sang it boldly for my Muslim friends:

I've got a river of life flowing out of me!
Makes the lame to walk, and the blind to see.
Opens prison doors, sets the captives free!

I've got a river of life flowing out of me!
Spring up, O well, within my soul!
Spring up, O well, and make me whole![123]

They clapped and cheered. I laughed but barely held back tears as I sensed the great honor of praying these words over them. The multiyear project was successful on all levels. The village women were freed from four-mile trips to get water each day, and God moved in lives. The River of Life as well as clean drinking water flowed down that mountain. The physical and spiritual needs of hundreds were addressed. Due to the gracious work of the engineer, along with the prayers and finances of the partners, villagers began to trust Jesus. Tom and I had much to celebrate with our friends and partners in North Africa, but there was another level of celebration when we returned to our church in America.

I participated in this partnership as the mission leader of a local church. This ministry partnership could just as easily have involved a family or a group of families that felt called to address physical and spiritual needs in Africa. Instead of the church—or in addition to it—families could have provided finances and prayer. Imagine you and your family sitting around those low tables, eating roast lamb, and celebrating God's goodness.

The purpose of these celebrations is to give gratitude to God and your partners, pray for the people being served, and discuss what you have learned about God, people, ministry, and yourself. The metrics might not be pretty, and your expectations might have been significantly unfulfilled. There will always be, however, something to celebrate.

Do It Again and Again

In addition to the annual evaluation, every day is an opportunity to review and celebrate your shining strategy. Don't be so bound to your plan that you miss the day-to-day lessons, holy moments, and subtle nudges to redirect the ministry.

After your annual celebration, it is time to start the lampstand building process over again. If the needs or your resources and life situation have changed (regarding a new family member, new job, health issues, or the like), adjust the plan. If your calling hasn't changed much and your methods are making progress toward your goals, you may choose to continue with the same strategy and partners. Reallocate resources and make other adjustments as necessary. Allow the lessons learned in year one to give direction to your future projects. The building process will go much faster since you have already established a baseline and understand the process.

Defining Characteristics of Tall Lampstands

Strategic living flows from an intentionality to be the best possible steward of God's blessings in order that the maximum number of lives are transformed and God is honored. Your lampstand and strategic approach to life and ministry will be uniquely yours, but here are some defining characteristics of all tall lampstands:[124]

> Motivated: Tall lampstands and strategic living are inspired by gratitude for God's kindness and driven by the desire to present an excellent gift to God.
> Integrated: Our commitment to shine is integrated into our daily lives as well as in the strategies to meet specific needs in our areas of focus.
> Informed: Our plans are guided by God's Word and use the most current information to find underserved needs and create tactics to address them.
> Apostolic: They avoid redundancy by giving priority to needs that are greatly underserved and to opportunities to share the good news with those who have limited access to the gospel.
> Holistic: They consider the diverse needs of people. Although one strategy may not be able to address all needs, a tall lampstand considers all vital needs, spiritual as well as temporal.

- ▸ Long-term: Although some needs are critical in nature and need immediate short-term attention, strategic ministries seek to make as much long-term impact as possible.
- ▸ Impactful: They prioritize tactics that promise to have a good return on investment and a significant ripple effect—the degree to which people and generations will be impacted beyond those initially involved.
- ▸ Spirit-led: They involve humility, intense prayer for the people served, and ongoing attention to the Spirit's guidance.
- ▸ Generous: They rely on the generous sharing of the participants' gifts and blessings to achieve the ministry goals.
- ▸ Relational: They build respectful and collaborative relationships with the people served as well as with other partners serving in the area.
- ▸ Christian: They clearly and graciously communicate the good news of Jesus—the reason for our work and the source of our compassion.
- ▸ Dated: They look toward the day when the ministry will no longer be needed or the ministry will be fully passed to the local population without creating dependency.

Execution

The merger between AOL and Time Warner in 2000 was the largest in business history at that time, but it ultimately failed. Steve Case, the CEO of AOL, later explained, "The execution didn't match the vision." Case then referenced the wisdom of Thomas Edison: "Vision without execution is hallucination."[125] Talk and good intentions are cheap. This chapter walked you through a series of steps to help you be more effective as the light of the world. Strategic Christians focus on shining every day, and they make the effort to build tall lampstands so their light shines far. The following chapters address factors that will either encourage or discourage your efforts to live faithfully as the light of the world.

Be the Change

CHAPTER 11: BUILDING A TALLER LAMPSTAND

Consider

> ➤ Think about the ways you shine for Jesus in your daily routines. How is that going?
> ➤ Consider these statements: "You want your prayers, time, and other resources to shine God's love as brightly as possible. You are determined to move beyond selfish and benevolent living." Rate yourself on a scale from 1 to 10, ranging from "absolutely does not apply to me" (1) to "absolutely applies to me" (10).

Interact

> ➤ Share which of the steps to build a taller lampstand are most needed in your journey right now.
> ➤ Does this model seem too complicated? If so, talk about a process that might better help you become more strategic.

Pray

> ➤ Thank God for calling and equipping you to be the light of the world.
> ➤ Thank Jesus for encouraging his disciples to build taller lampstands. Ask the Spirit to guide you as you move from "high-sounding words" to action.
> ➤ Pray for Christ followers who are developing more effective ways to minister to the underserved and unreached in your neighborhood and far beyond.

Act

> ‣ Open a new file in your computer or get a new notebook. Review the steps to build a taller lampstand, and follow the directions for step one and two. Do more if time allows.
> ‣ If you want help in developing your personal plan to shine, please email the author or visit the *Born to Shine* website.

C H A P T E R   1 2

An Excellent Gift

Aware of this, Jesus said to them, "Why are you bothering this woman? She has done a beautiful thing to me."

—Matthew 26:10

Highlights

> The Bible is full of stories about people presenting excellent gifts to the Lord as a response to God's holiness and grace.

> In contrast to perfection, excellence is not determined by the absence of flaws, imperfections, or sins. The faith and motivation of the giver are what make a gift excellent.

> The strategic seek to shine with excellence so the maximum number of lives may be freed from darkness and God receives glory.

When have you seen or experienced excellence lately? After having cataract surgery at the Callahan Eye Hospital in Alabama, I can attest to the excellence of their entire system. I was moved by the young, passionate worship dancers in a service at Abundant Grace International Fellowship in Shanghai. They were excellent. The superstars of professional sports routinely perform physical feats that are breathtakingly excellent. The staff and volunteers at New Life Mission in Florida exhibit excellence every day as they serve homeless moms with joy and empower families to be self-sufficient. In the food category, I appreciate the hotpot restaurant in China called Hai Di Lao. It has friendly and prompt service, healthy and delicious food, and a wonderful environment. It is excellent.

We have all had glimpses of excellence, but each of our earthbound examples is relative and temporary. We mere mortals can perform in ways that might be described as excellent, but only God is perfect. Everything about God is perfect. When we appropriately recognize God's perfect power, glory, and grace, we yearn to offer him our best and highest efforts.

The Theme of Excellence

Here are a few New Testament verses that relate to excellence and our calling to offer God our best:

> Jesus replied: "Love the Lord your God with all your heart and with all your soul and with all your mind." (Matthew 22:37)

> Since you are eager for gifts of the Spirit, try to excel in those that build up the church. (1 Corinthians 14:12)

> But just as you excel in everything—in faith, in speech, in knowledge, in complete earnestness and in your love for us—see that you also excel in this grace of giving. (2 Corinthians 8:7)

> Finally, brothers and sisters, whatever is true, whatever is noble, whatever is right, whatever is pure, whatever is lovely, whatever is admirable—if anything is excellent or praiseworthy—think about such things. (Philippians 4:8)

> Whatever you do, work heartily, as for the Lord and not for men, knowing that from the Lord you will receive

the inheritance as your reward. You are serving the Lord Christ. (Colossians 3:23–24 ESV)

Those who have served well gain an excellent standing and great assurance in their faith in Christ Jesus. (1 Timothy 3:13)

The theme of excellence also flows through the Old Testament. Consider the sacrificial system. The books of Exodus, Leviticus, and Numbers use the same words to describe animals chosen as offerings to God: "without blemish." These two words pointed toward that one perfect Sacrifice that was to come. God's law called for the worshipper to present a gift to God that was as close to perfect as possible. The call was for excellence.

Consider the tabernacle and the temple. God provided the designs for the architecture, furnishings, and functions. These designs communicated realities about the Creator's nature, our need, and the coming Messiah, who would provide a new and living way for us to relate to God (Hebrews 7:18–19; 10:20). Moses, David, and Solomon were careful to implement God's designs and conscripted the world's best workers with wood, gold, silver, bronze, linen, and more. Their goal was excellence.

After describing all that Moses should make for the Tabernacle, God concluded by saying, "And look that you make them after their pattern, which was showed you in the mount" (Exodus 25:40). Moses oversaw the construction according to that pattern (Hebrews 8:5). Upon completion of the Tabernacle, Moses gave the final inspection and "saw that they had done it just as the Lord had commanded" (Exodus 39:43). Excellence.

God gave King David a detailed plan for the temple. Although God prevented him from building the temple, David began to gather all the materials that would be needed. David later commissioned his son Solomon to complete the task in a way worthy of the Designer. "Take heed now; for the Lord hath chosen you to build a house for the sanctuary: be strong and do it" (1 Chronicles 28:9–10). King Solomon's workers took seven years to construct the temple according to those plans. It was magnificent. Excellence.

Consider Jesus's response to the woman who anointed him with costly perfume (Matthew 26:6–13; Mark 14:3–9; Luke 7:36–50). Although neither his disciples nor other onlookers appreciated the act, Jesus received the extravagant gift graciously. He acknowledged that sincere love and gratitude prompted the offering (Luke 7:47). In Mark 14:6, we find a key motivation for strategic living. We want to offer a gift to Jesus that he will esteem as excellent. Trying to help the disciples understand the woman's offering, Jesus commented, "She has done a beautiful thing to me."

Moses, David, Solomon, and this woman knew that the God of the universe deserves the best, finest, and choicest offerings. No matter how costly, extravagant, or excellent the gift, it is well-deserved by the Lord of lords. God is worthy. The purpose of this chapter is to connect the concept of excellence with our role as the light of the world. Excellence is the overarching reason one might go through the hassle of developing an intentional lifestyle to shine brightly. We are strategic because we want our gift to God to be excellent. Since we sincerely love Jesus and he is worthy of the most excellent praise, we do whatever it takes to present him with beautiful gifts.

I heard this desire in the voice of my friend Jacob in Asia. His ministry supervisor had placed him in a challenging situation but provided Jacob with little training or support for his efforts to equip young pastors. One day Jacob confessed that it had been another hard week. He felt alone, less than effective, and frustrated. After a long sigh, he said, "I just want to do it well! God deserves my best." Excellence.

Perfection

Perfection and related concepts are used frequently in Scripture. Jesus challenged, "Be perfect, therefore, as your heavenly Father is perfect" (Matthew 5:48). He asked a rich man if he wanted to be perfect (Matthew 19:21). In Romans 12:1–2 Paul challenges Christians: "Do not conform to the pattern of this world, but be transformed by the renewing of your mind. Then you will be able to test and approve what God's will is—his good, pleasing and perfect will." In calling the Corinthians to deeper faith and love, Paul appealed to them to "be perfectly united in mind and thought" (1 Corinthians 1:10), and he encouraged them: "Let us purify ourselves from everything that contaminates body and spirit, perfecting holiness out of reverence for God" (2 Corinthians 7:1).

Verses like these may cause confusion about the difference between *being* and *doing*, who we are and what we do as God's children. Our being as the children of God is not based on our performance, perfection, excellence, or shining. Our being is rooted solely in Jesus. The perfect work of Christ on Calvary washes us clean and makes us holy (sanctified). Jesus spoke this truth to Paul: "I am sending you to them to open their eyes and turn them from darkness to light, and from the power of Satan to God, so that they may receive forgiveness of sins and a place among those who are sanctified by faith in me" (Acts 26:17–18). Once we are children of faith (being), the Holy Spirit continues to work in us, guiding, empowering, comforting, teaching, and shaping us into the men and women God desires us to be. This sanctifying work of God produces a desire to please our Savior, to make God known, and to grow in grace. Paul thus declares, "I press on toward the goal to win the prize for which God has called me heavenward in Christ Jesus" (Philippians 3:14). Because we are God's forgiven children (being), we seek to bring excellent gifts to God (doing).

The Heart Determines Excellence

Excellence is not the same as perfection. It is not determined by the absence of flaws, imperfections, or sins. Neither is it a badge awarded to the one who has done more than others. The motivation and heart of the giver are what make a gift excellent. It is not the relative perfection of the effort or the gift itself. Unless the worshipper is giving in faith with a pure, loving, thankful, and repentant heart, the gift will be meaningless and perhaps nothing more than an attempt to appease holy God or buy a blessing. The faith chapter in Hebrews tells us that without faith it is impossible to please God (Hebrews 11:6). When Abraham offered his son Isaac, he did so in faith, and God affirmed his offering with the words "Now I know that you fear God, because you have not withheld from me your son, your only son" (Genesis 22:2–3, 12). In faith and love, Abraham offered the most treasured gift possible. His offering was excellent.

When Jesus saw the widow offer two small copper coins, worth only a few cents, he recognized her gift as excellent (Mark 12:42–44). Her gift was far smaller than the gifts of others, but she gave sacrificially, putting in everything she had to live on. She gave in faith and in deep gratitude. She knew that God deserved her best.

David was a mere shepherd boy who was willing to bring a rock to a sword fight with the giant Goliath. He had practiced. He had checked his sling. He took care to select the best stones for his task. He prayed and probably sang as he girded up his faith to offer his life for God's glory. As a young boy, he didn't think he had much to offer, but he gave his best.

Humanly speaking, I've never been accused of being excellent at anything. I am the epitome of the saying "jack of all trades, master of none." But I have been part of some excellent efforts. I was in a Christian band during my college years. We were young Christians excited to share the gospel. Our use of drums, guitars, a keyboard, and big speakers in churches and parking lots across the Southeast drew the attention of young and old. We did our best to belt out the music of artists like the Archers, Jimmy Owens, and Andraé Crouch. There were at most four true musicians in the group of twelve. The rest of us prayed, shared, and made a joyful noise. We were students in four universities across Mississippi, but we came together weekly for practice, prayer, and Bible study. Neither our music nor our message was perfect, but our effort was excellent. People responded to our invitations to follow Jesus. It seemed that God was pleased with our imperfect but sincere offering.

What about you? Take a minute to remember something you have attempted or achieved that you feel represents excellence although it probably wasn't perfect.

The Controversy of Excellence

A discussion of excellence can create tension. The excellent efforts of one worker, student, performer, or athlete may put an unwelcome spotlight on the unexceptional efforts of their peers. Some people disagree with the amount of time, energy, and resources required to achieve excellence. Others feel that excellence is unnecessary, misdirected, or impossible. This may have been the attitude of the disciples when they witnessed the beautiful but costly anointing of Jesus (Matthew 26:6–13; Mark 14:3–9; Luke 7:36–50). What one sees as a beautiful gift for God others see as a waste.

I understand the need for caution. A commitment to excellence can be confused with or become a form of perfectionism. I am not recommending perfectionism in any way. Unchecked perfectionism cripples relationships and crushes the spirits of those who may already feel inferior. Perfectionism can also be the enemy of progress. We can use our desire to "get things right" as an excuse for slow progress or inaction. There are many times when expedience needs to overrule excellence in the normal course of life, but when it comes to responding to God's grace, excellence is an appropriate desire. In the process of building a taller lampstand, we need balance. It's not helpful to overthink the process but jumping too quickly is equally unwise. Our challenge is to make *strategic* decisions—timely choices that utilize available resources and bring a maximum return on investment. This commitment to excellence requires hard work and a patience that never disconnects with the urgent needs of people. As the recipients of God's grace, we want to do our best (which is never perfection), and we want to act as quickly as possible. This is part of what it means to do something beautiful for God.

Good Enough

God's children have always had temptations to stop short of excellence. God blessed Abraham and his descendants and gave them a mission to bless the world. Eventually their global calling was trumped by selfishness. They stopped short of their calling. They settled for less than excellence. "It is too small a thing that you should be my servant to raise up the tribes of Jacob … I will give you as a light to the Gentiles, that my salvation may reach to the end of the earth" (Isaiah 49:6). To bless only their own ethnic group, the tribes of Jacob, was a good thing, but it was not good enough when God's calling was to bless the Gentiles as well as Jews.

In decision-making, we might assume that there are four options: excellent, good, good enough, and bad. No one intentionally makes a bad decision, and excellent decisions may seem unlikely if not impossible. In most cases, the masses are satisfied with making decisions that are good or good enough. In 2019, AT&T began to use a humorous and effective advertising campaign that related to this reality in our culture. The television ads depicted situations where "just OK was not OK." No one would want a surgeon deemed to be just okay. No one would choose a babysitter that's just okay, and the thought of eating sushi that's just okay makes me queasy. We tend to use the qualifier "good enough" only when the decision has little impact on our own lives. The words "good enough" and "just okay" are appropriate filters when we are buying socks or deciding which movie to watch, but not when it comes to the stewardship of our lives. *Good* is often not good enough. Shall we work with haste for an end to all racism, cancer, war, and ignorance of the gospel, or is it good enough for us to only seek partial and slow remedies for these challenges?

Consider again how God sees our gifts. An imperfect offering that represents the best efforts of a sincere worshipper is excellent. If, however, a person knowingly offers God less than his best, God may consider this stealing. "'Cursed is the cheat who has an acceptable male in his flock and vows to give it, but then sacrifices a blemished animal to the Lord. For I am a great king,' says the Lord Almighty" (Malachi 1:13b–14). The words "good enough" find little room in the heart of a redeemed sinner considering how to use his or her resources to bless God and bless the world.

An Excellent Lampstand

Here's an example of a group that is dedicated to excellence. Short-term mission trips became more and more common in the 1980s. People continue to love these opportunities to serve in a foreign culture for a few days or weeks. Many local churches have made these short missions the backbone of their outreach strategy. Over the years, however, many sending churches and missionaries who hosted teams began to notice a sad disconnect. Although passionate and full of good intentions, many teams were ineffective or worse. Instead of advancing the ministry goals of the hosting church or organization, many groups distracted the local workers and caused problems that took weeks to unravel. In 2003, Standards of Excellence in Short-Term Mission (SOE) was launched to assist "mission sending and receiving entities in pursuing excellence for effective Kingdom service."[126] Instead of settling for good enough, churches that apply the seven standards of excellence to their mission trips lift the light of Christ much higher. With good training, collaboration, preparation, and planning, every short-term mission can be excellent. It takes desire and hard work to present an excellent offering to our perfect God.

We experience God's grace in an infinite number of blessings, but one is preeminent. The Father gave his best—the Son of God—as the once-and-for-all redemptive gift for humankind. That is excellence to an infinite degree. It is the perfect gift. The opening scene in the 1998 movie version of Victor Hugo 's *Les Misérables* points to the excellence of God's offering and our response in faith. The convict Jean Valjean is affronted by the shocking generosity of Monseigneur Bienvenu. Even after Valjean attacks him and steals the church's silverware, the priest refuses to press charges with the police. He even offers Valjean more silver. In response to the tough convict's request for an explanation, Bienvenu says, "Jean Valjean, my brother, you no longer belong to evil. With this silver, I've bought your soul. I've ransomed you from fear and hatred. Now I give you back to God."[127] The gift of the priest was costly—silver and his own blood. The priest's motivation was pure, and his sacrifice was redemptive. His excellent offering illuminated the perfect grace of God as seen in Jesus Christ. Bienvenu did something beautiful for God by offering broken and sinful Jean Valjean grace and hope. As we lift high our lanterns as strategic Christians, we love others in the way God has loved us—with excellence.

In Matthew 22, Jesus shares that the second-greatest commandment is to "love your neighbor as yourself" (39). In the Gospel of John, Jesus clarifies what it means to love our neighbors. He calls us to have the same type sacrificial, excellent love that he demonstrated. "As I have loved you, so you must love one another" (John 13:34). God's gracious and excellent movement toward us is an invitation to respond in faith, gratitude, and a life of service to others. That is part of the message of Maxie Dunnam's book *The Intercessory Life*. Because Christ abides in us, we can be and do for others what God has been and done for us. As we reflect on God's grace and remember Christ's abiding presence, our hearts burst with gratitude and the Spirit gives us the desire to shine brightly.

Perhaps you have decided not to live in the sad land of selfishness or even the good land of benevolence. Because of your desire to bring great glory to God and transformation to hurting and lost people, you intend to live strategically. You are, therefore, thinking carefully about how to invest the resources of your life. You want to build an excellent lampstand. As you build, remember to avoid the two extremes: (1) the trap of perfectionism that will bog you down and frustrate progress, and (2) the allure to settle for "good enough" when the need, your ability, and God's worth call for much more. Find balance. Don't overthink the process, but don't jump too quickly. An appropriate gift for the love of your life takes effort.

Standing Ovations

Speaking of the wonderful variety of God's gifts, William Wilberforce said, "We have different forms assigned to us in the school of life, different gifts imparted. All is not attractive that is good. Iron is useful, though it does not sparkle like the diamond. Gold has not the fragrance of a flower. So different persons have various modes of excellence, and we must have an eye to all."[128] Although the details of your excellent shining will be quite different from your neighbor's or your church's, your motivation will be similar. All bright lights are driven by a passion to offer God our best.

Clive Calver told a story about a remarkable young pianist who was given a chance to perform a concert in front of a huge crowd. That night he played Bach with uncommon brilliance and passion. As he finished and left the stage, the crowd rose in a spontaneous standing ovation. The concert promoter urged the pianist to go back out and play an encore, but the boy responded, "No. There's a man in the third row in the balcony. He's not standing. He's my teacher. If he were standing and everyone else was sitting, I would play an encore. But because he is sitting, no encore."[129] Regardless of what other people think, students understand their debt of gratitude to their teacher, and they naturally and primarily seek to please their master.

We see this dynamic played out in a different way in Luke's description of Stephen's death in Acts 7:54–60. As he was being stoned, Stephen's face lit up and shone brightly as he saw Jesus waiting for him in glory. Interestingly, the text says that Jesus was standing at the right hand of God, in contrast to other biblical images that portray Christ sitting at the right hand of Father God. It seems that Christ was standing in acknowledgment of a life well-lived. The teacher was pleased, and Stephen soon heard the words we all hope to hear: "'Well done, good and faithful servant." (Matthew 25:21).

When a guest approaches his or her host to present a gift of gratitude, the host stands. It is not the quality of the gift that determines the receptive posture of the host. The host stands to acknowledge that a price has been paid, energy has been exerted, and the giver has tried his best to please the host. We are motivated to build taller lampstands and live strategically because God is honored by our efforts to present gifts of excellence.

Be the Change

CHAPTER 12: AN EXCELLENT GIFT

Consider

> ➤ Think about the most recent time you thought or said something like "Wow. That was excellent!"

- When is excellence a priority for you? Consider areas like your time at work, your performance in sports or in the kitchen, the academic performance of your children, your financial investments, and your pastor's sermons.
- In what ways does excellence apply to the way you shine?

Interact

- Share about your understanding of the difference between excellence and perfectionism.
- Talk about situations in your life when good enough is okay and when is it not okay.

Pray

- Thank God for the perfection of the holy Trinity, heaven, and our salvation in Christ.
- Give thanks for your desire to offer God an excellent gift of gratitude. Ask God to help you live in such a way that you will someday hear the words "Well done" from the Creator of the universe.
- Pray for musicians and songwriters who are creating excellent music and other tools that move us to worship and witness.

Act

- Thank someone for demonstrating excellence in the way he or she shines for Jesus.
- List three ways your shining can be more excellent this week.

CHAPTER 13

God Is Worth It

When the trumpets sounded, the army shouted, and at the sound of
the trumpet, when the men gave a loud shout, the wall collapsed;
so everyone charged straight in, and they took the city.

—Joshua 6:20

Highlights

> God is worthy of excellence and is honored by our efforts to
  present gifts of excellence.
> Living a life "worthy of the Lord" includes a growing faith and
  diligence in blessing others with the love of God.
> Living strategically involves more than hoping and praying that
  our impact on the world will grow. It takes stamina, courage,
  and hard work.

Wulongshan, or Five Dragon Mountain, in Northeast China is not the
type of mountain that forces climbers to use oxygen tanks and Sherpas.
It was, however, a good challenge for me on a cold morning in 2018. I
had made great progress by noon and stopped to rest and hydrate. I
was alone but determined. I was tired but not exhausted. I was cold
even before the clouds began to release sleet and snow, but I pressed

on. I badly wanted to summit for two reasons. First, I pushed forward because of something in my DNA. I have always been passionate about seeing what is around the corner, at the end of the trail, at the top of the mountain. And second, I wanted to be prepared to guide my friends and family who would join me on this trek in the following months.

As I continued to ascend, the ice began to accumulate on the rocks, trail, and ironworks installed to help climbers. It was increasingly slippery, and the temperature kept dropping. More than once I asked myself, "Should I go on?" Each time, something inside me answered affirmatively. Although the clouds and precipitation blocked my view of the mountaintop, I felt that I was close. I pressed on.

After not seeing another person for hours, I heard voices and finally saw a couple descending the mountain. When we met on the trail, they seemed surprised to see me. They offered me some fruit, and I offered them a granola bar. After talking for a few minutes in limited English and Chinese, I asked if they had made it to the summit. The man nodded and replied with a victorious "Yes." He then pointed up the mountain and asked, "You?" I shrugged, laughed, and asked them, "Was it worth it?" They laughed loudly, patted me on the back, and continued down the mountain. Alone again in the snowy wilderness, I strained to catch a glimpse of the peak as I wondered aloud: "Is this worth it?" Reality began to sink in. *I am alone. My phone has no signal. My friends and coworkers are one hundred miles away, and they know little about my hiking plans. The temperature is dropping. The wind and ice are increasing, but … I'm almost there. I've come this far. It wouldn't be wise for me to take others up a mountain that I have not summited.* I pressed on.

Thirty minutes later, the wind blew the clouds back for a moment, and I looked up, hoping to get a view of the summit. Although I could see hundreds of feet farther up the mountain, the peak was still out of sight. I gulped down warm water and asked myself again, "Is it worth the risk?"[130]

This chapter is meant to help you push through the natural hesitancy to reclaim your identity as the light of the world and begin living strategically. By now you have said to yourself: "Yikes. This will not be easy." Every child of God who has considered shining more brightly has asked, "Is shining more brightly worth the effort?"

What is God Worth?

English speakers are fond of using expressions that include the words "worth" or "worthy." I found 137 idioms using these words. Here is a sampling:[131]

- ‣ A picture is worth a thousand words.
- ‣ Anyone worth his or her salt …
- ‣ Be worth one's weight in gold
- ‣ Do something for all you are worth
- ‣ If a thing is worth doing, it's worth doing well.
- ‣ Not worth the trouble.

The words "worth" and "worthy" are also frequently used in the Bible. There are many references to God as being worthy of praise (1 Chronicles 16:25; 2 Samuel 22:4; Psalms 18:3; 48:1; 96:4; 145:3; Hebrews 3:3; Revelation 4:11). John uses the word as he tries to describe the climax of history: "In a loud voice they were saying: 'Worthy is the Lamb, who was slain, to receive power and wealth and wisdom and strength and honor and glory and praise!'" (Revelation 5:12). God is worthy of our praise and far more.

The Bible speaks of those who are not worthy and those who are worthy. John the Baptist told Jesus that he was not worthy to untie Jesus's sandals (John 1:27). The prodigal acknowledged that he was not worthy to be called a son (Luke 15:21). Anyone who loves family more than Jesus (Matthew 10:37) and anyone who does not take up his cross and follow Jesus (Matthew 10:38) is not worthy of Jesus. In John's vision of the age to come, no one was found worthy to untie and read the scroll (Revelation 5:4). Those who trust and faithfully follow Jesus are described as being worthy of the kingdom (2 Thessalonians 1:5), worthy of the gospel of Christ (Philippians 1:27), worthy of his calling (Ephesians 4:1; 2 Thessalonians 1:11), and worthy of taking part in the age to come and in the resurrection (Luke 20:35). In Colossians 1:10, Paul prays that the believers in Colossae might "live a life worthy of the Lord and please him in every way: bearing fruit in every good work, growing in the knowledge of God."

God is worthy of our best offerings, our best efforts, and our highest and brightest shining. We are saved by faith through the grace of God, and it is our joy to spend the rest of our lives demonstrating our gratitude. Living a life "worthy of the Lord" involves an abiding faith and diligence in blessing others with the love of God. A life that has a massive impact on the world with God's love, however, is not the result of hoping or good luck. It takes intentionality, stamina, courage, and hard work.

Our Utmost for God's Highest

History is full of examples of hard work and perseverance reaping world-changing breakthroughs. In 1879, Thomas Edison patented an effective incandescent lightbulb that some said would banish darkness forever. Like many pioneers, he knew that success and excellence would be costly. Edison tested over six thousand elements from across the world in search of the most suitable filament material. Regarding the cost of time and energy, he wrote, "I was never myself discouraged, or inclined to be hopeless of success. I cannot say the same for all my associates."[132] Recalling the successful flight of the Wright brothers in 1903, one observer commented, "It wasn't luck that made them fly; it was hard work and common sense; they put their whole heart and soul and all their energy into an idea and they had the faith."[133] Wilbur and Orville were inspired. They were smart. They felt called. They worked hard. They had faith, and they were willing to risk everything to fulfill their vision of flight. World-changing breakthroughs require determination, sacrifice, and hard work.

I imagine that—not unlike Edison, the Wright brothers, and other pioneers—you feel a degree of inspiration and calling to "soar on wings like eagles" (Isaiah 40:31). You, too, want to make an impact. You want to lift your lantern high. You want to live a life worthy of your calling because God is worthy. And yet you tremble at the prospect. You have realized that a life that brings God glory and impacts lives on the highest levels requires an immense amount of sweat. Being self-centered takes almost no energy; it comes naturally. Being benevolent takes some effort, but often not much. Being strategic takes hard work, focus, time, and a commitment to not let the benevolent masses lull us into the easier style of nonstrategic living.

A sports analogy might help us better see the foolishness of pursuing a goal without a commitment to sweating or joining a team, but living in a way that is not worthy of the uniform. Across the United States, Friday nights in the fall are reserved for one activity. Churches and businesses do their best to not conflict with this tradition. Thousands of fans show up to cheer for their high school teams as they attempt to score more points than the opposition in the game Americans call football. In one sense, football is a simple game. It is merely one team trying to get an oddly shaped leather ball across their goal line more times than their opponent. With such a simple goal, try to imagine the following scenario. I call this team "Loftin's Losers."

> The players and coaches on the team do not prepare. There are no sweaty practices and no boring study sessions to learn their opponent's tendencies.
> No thought is given to the assignment of duties. Since the game is so simple, the players just rotate positions.
> There is no game plan. Coach Loftin tells his team, "Just do what feels right."

Although I have cheered for some football teams that seemed to have this approach, a "nonstrategy strategy" usually does not produce success. Marv Levy, former Hall of Fame coach of the Buffalo Bills, was known for his strategic leadership. Levy said, "What it takes to win is simple, but it is not easy." The simple task of taking a football across the goal line more often than your opponent requires hours of tactical planning and preparation. It takes work.

As members of God's family, God's team, we have been given a mission that could be considered simple: love God and demonstrate

God's love to the world. The mission is huge and urgent. A haphazard response to the mission does not align with its importance to God. This assignment requires our best effort. This is the response described by the title of Oswald Chambers's classic devotional *Our Utmost for His Highest*. Those who want to participate with maximum effort—those children of God who desire to lift their lanterns high—will be sure to pray as well as plan, prepare, count the cost, and follow through. This is true for any important mission, including rearing children, growing a business, or planting a church. Faithfulness requires more than good intentions and haphazard attempts.

Unfortunately, our tendency is to function like the laid-back Loftin's Losers, who just hope for the best. This approach to light-bearing does not make us bad people. It does not mean we don't desire to do good things. It does not mean we are blind to the needs of the world. And it has nothing to do with God continuing to love us. When we yield to this haphazard approach to our mission, we are hoping to bring excellence to God without a plan and without sweating much. Hope is our plan.

In Matthew 5, Jesus seems to acknowledge this tendency in his followers. After establishing the fact that his followers are the light of the world, Jesus sees the need to caution them about not putting their light under a bowl. We are in good company. Many before us and around us now are content not to lift their lights high. Take a moment, however, to recall your mom's or dad's response when you tried to justify some behavior with the plea "Everybody is doing it." I well-remember my mother's pointed reply: "Would you put your hand in a fire or jump off a cliff just because your friends do? Think, son. Remember who you are."

Beyond a Will to Win

As we honestly compare our shining to the calling of Jesus, the truth becomes obvious. We pledge our allegiance to the King of light, but often our shining lacks passion and is less effective than it could be. "Excellent" is rarely the best word to describe the shining of many Christ followers and churches. Our default style is to take the easier path. In what arenas of life does a laid-back style produce excellence or victory? Legendary University of Alabama football coach Paul "Bear" Bryant preached that the commitment to prepare is the key to winning. Everyone wants to win, but victors consistently put in hours of sweaty work well before gameday. In athletics, business, the arts, and Christian witness, one's work ethic is a key factor in reaching goals. The absence of a commitment to prepare to shine indicates an underappreciation of our mission and a lack of loyalty to the One who calls us.

Here is my point. Our tendency is to enjoy God's blessings without giving much consideration to how we can shine more brightly. Without significant preparation, planning, and execution, our desire to change the world with God's love will produce ineffectiveness and frustration. As a result, our joy in being the light of the world is tempered by thoughts like these:

> Regardless of how much I do for God, I feel like I'm not doing enough.
> I feel guilty when I hear others talk about how they are trying to change the world.
> I feel paralyzed when I receive an invitation to help with another good cause. There are too many needs. I have no idea what to do.
> I feel that my outreach efforts are scattered and have little impact.
> I'm frustrated about not being able to explain why I address certain needs and ignore others.

If you relate to one or more of these statements, God may be creating a holy discontentment in your soul. Frustration has trumped the joy you should feel about reflecting God's light in the world. There is a way to serve Christ that brings contentment to our souls. In his book on joy as a theme for ministry, David F. White writes, "To reclaim joy, is to retrieve a practicable virtue of the Christian faith, a practice that involves attending to gratitude for God's gracious gifts, which potentially moves us to worship and empowers us for active love of God and neighbor."[134] There is joy in heaven and in our souls when we reclaim our identity as the light of the world. That is what this book is about. That is why you are still reading. You want to be moved to worship God and love others with more excellence. You desire to lift your lantern higher. It will take consistent intentionality and hard work. That is the way it has always been.

Why the Jericho Mission Succeeded

One example of God's mission strategy is found in Joshua 5:13–6:5. The people of God were on their way to the Promised Land, but a huge obstacle blocked their path—the strategically important and well-fortified city of Jericho. God, however, had a plan. The Lord gave Joshua specific instructions on how to be victorious in overcoming the city. The children of Abraham were directed to march around the walls of the city once every day for six days. On the seventh day, they were to march around the wall seven times. On the last lap, the priests were instructed to blow their horns, and the other Israelites were to give a great shout. At that point, God promised to bring down the walls of Jericho, allowing the Israelites to easily take the city. God's plan for victory involved a human–Divine partnership. God could have said, "Joshua, you and the people only need to sit and watch. I will knock the walls down." Although their help was not needed, God wanted the people to be intimately involved in the mission. The people of faith were part of God's plan. The King of Kings invited them to sweat. They responded in faith and obedience, and I imagine that the marching, trumpeting, and shouting by the Israelites was done with power, precision, and passion. God's plan miraculously provided victory for the Israelites and brought great glory to God.

Hundreds of years after the walls of Jericho fell, the Bible introduces Nehemiah, a central figure in a saga regarding the walls of another city. Hearing that the walls of Jerusalem were still in rubble after the Babylonians demolished the city, Nehemiah asked God for the privilege of rebuilding the walls. The poor shape of Jerusalem dishonored God and rebuilding the walls was the first step in recovery. After being commissioned by God as well as King Artaxerxes, Nehemiah created a strategic plan and moved forward. This was a huge task with numerous challenges. Nehemiah faced ridicule, intimidation, problems within the camp, and political maneuvering as he and his team put one brick on top of another (Nehemiah 3:15–5:13). Commenting on the obstacles Nehemiah and all God's people face when we move forward to fulfill our calling and mission, Brian Hardin said, "The dream was awesome, but the blood and sweat of trying to make it happen is difficult."[135] Nehemiah saw a need, volunteered to address the need, received God's blessing, developed a plan, and pushed through all threats to complete the mission.

Great Gifts, Great Cost

Victory in any mission we undertake with and for Jesus is not achieved without God's grace and our perseverance. Our tendency to be selfish, however, can woo us to merely sing Christian choruses from our comfortable couches, a lifestyle that does little to shine the light of Christ on the world. Admitting his early self-centered values, William Wilberforce confessed, "The first years in Parliament I did nothing—nothing to any purpose. My own distinction was my darling object."[136] He grew depressed about his life of selfishness, but everything changed in 1786 when he had a transforming experience with Christ. As he grew in the faith, Wilberforce came to understand that God had given him great blessings so he could make a difference in the world, and he eventually took up the cause of ending slave trade. "So enormous, so dreadful, so irremediable did the trade's wickedness appear that my own mind was completely made up for abolition. Let the consequences be what they would: I from this time determined that I would never rest until I had effected its abolition."[137] Wilberforce battled poor health and bitter resistance from almost every politician, business leader, friend, and family member. He proposed bill after bill to Parliament, only to see them defeated; but in 1807, his perseverance was rewarded. It took almost twenty years of hard work, but Parliament finally passed a bill to abolish the slave trade in the British Empire. William Wilberforce lifted the light of Christ in such a way that thousands of people experienced freedom. Wilberforce persevered.

Wilberforce is one of many who have fought to tear down the walls of racism and injustice throughout history. *Twelve Years a Slave* is the memoir of Solomon Northup (1807–1863) that was made into a movie by that name in 2013. Born free, Solomon was a successful African American businessman, musician, and family man in New York. In 1841, he was kidnapped and sold into slavery. Northup worked on plantations in Louisiana for twelve years before being freed by the efforts of Samuel Bass, a carpenter who was covertly fighting for the abolition of slavery. Mr. Bass's compassion, integrity, hard work, good planning, and courage provided for the freedom and salvation of Northup.

Wilberforce and Bass were bright lights lifted high for Christ and for the good of the world. Both followed a strategy, worked hard, and took risks. Bass changed the lives of a man and his family, but Wilberforce changed a nation and the lives of thousands who would have suffered in slavery. Both followed the assignment God gave them. Both are heroes. Both offered an excellent gift to God. But if I had a choice and God gave me the opportunity and power, I would rather make an impact on the scale of Wilberforce's. I expect that Bass would have chosen that option also. I compare these two great people to illustrate the natural desire of a healthy and balanced child of God. We want to honor God and bless the world to the greatest degree possible.

Every Christ follower is part of God's mysterious method to redeem and transform the world. Each of us is invited to work with God in tearing down the walls of brokenness, shame, injustice, poverty, and sin. We are called to demonstrate and proclaim the good news of God's love to the world. We are called to lift our lanterns high. Shining in a way that changes lives and transforms nations requires intentional effort. It takes courage, hard work, sweat, and patience. Even our best, however, is not enough. Our excellence is nothing unless it is blessed and empowered by God. I appreciate the distinction made by Chris Hodges: "Prayer is the difference between the best I can do, and the best God can do."[138] Victory is normally facilitated by our work and God's power. "By faith the walls of Jericho fell, after the people had marched around them for seven days" (Hebrews 11:30).

Perhaps you are wondering if living strategically is a mountain trek that is worth the blood, sweat and tears it will cost you. Center your soul by answering this question: Is God worthy of your best effort?

Be the Change

CHAPTER 13: GOD IS WORTH IT

Consider

> ➤ Think about the subconscious assumptions you have had about the Christian life.
> ➤ Did you think faithfulness to Christ would be easy? Did you think it would come naturally? Did you think you would grow without intentionality? Do you think you can shine more brightly without taking some risks and paying a price?

Interact

> ➤ Share about something you have achieved that cost you greatly— something that required hard work or significant resources.
> ➤ Why is it easy to assume that shining for Christ should just happen when everything else that is important in life takes preparation, effort, resources, and risk?

Pray

> ➤ Thank God for being patient with you. Ask the Spirit to give you courage and determination to persevere in shining brightly for God's glory.
> ➤ Thank God for the saints who took great risks to bring the good news to your continent.
> ➤ Pray for those who are serving children and youth around the world.

Act

> ➤ Write down two ways you can put more energy and sweat into the ways you can shine this week?
> ➤ Continue working on the list of steps to build a taller lampstand for Jesus.

CHAPTER 14

Basket Cases

You are the light of the world. A city set on a hill cannot be hidden.
Nor do people light a lamp and put it under a basket.

—Matthew 5:15 ESV

Highlights

> Flawed thinking undercuts our attempts to live strategically by creating baskets that limit our shining.

> Flawed thinking can be caused by the wounds of life, the influence of the selfish and benevolent, or a deficiency in our knowledge of scripture and the needs of the world.

> Here is guidance to identify and cast off light-blocking baskets so our lives will better reflect God's light and love.

Perhaps you have decided to become a more strategic light for Christ. You know God is worthy of your best efforts. But you are not naive. You realize that shining brightly will take hard work and you will encounter many distractions and hurdles. God may have transformed your attitude about shining, but it is easy to slide back into styles of shining that are less than bright or strategic. The next two chapters provide suggestions that will help you resist that tendency.

The language of Matthew 5:15 suggests that it is impossible for a city to completely hide its glow and unlikely that a person will intentionally limit the light emanating from his or her lamp. A person who doesn't have flawed thinking will not choose to limit their light. All of us, however, have flawed thinking at times. We act in ways that are not aligned with the character of God due to sin, the scars on our souls caused by our own words and deeds or those of others, the influence of the selfish and benevolent around us, or a deficiency in our knowledge of scripture and the needs of the world. For one reason or another, consciously or unconsciously, we sometimes allow baskets to cover our lanterns.

Jonathan and I were sound asleep in our tent until 2:00 a.m. He heard the noises before I did. Long howls and the pounding of many small feet. A pack of coyotes seemed to be excited about encircling our tent. I grabbed my powerful Maglite hoping that its bright light and my screams would encourage the pack to play elsewhere. My scream was impressive, but the flashlight produced nothing but a mellow yellow glow. Suddenly I realized what was wrong. I had dropped the light on the trail, and I'd forgotten to clean it. The lens was caked in dried mud. I was armed with a powerful light, but its impact was blocked because of my neglect.

Christ followers who don't shine brightly may have many righteous priorities, but something is amiss in their lives. Their lamps are burning, but the light is partially blocked. They may have been bright strategic lights in the past, but now their lives only emit a dim glow. We all encounter light-blocking attitudes at various times in our lives. All the baskets below are real, but none are so heavy that you and the Holy Spirit cannot remove them from your lamp.

1. Stuck

Life is a series of seasons. Some are wonderful; others are challenging. Some bring freedom; others bring restrictions. For a season, your family situation was more complicated than it had been. For a season, you were extremely busy with work duties, or you were unemployed. For a season, you fought an illness or served the health needs of a family member. For a season, you lived in a country where Christian witness is greatly limited by the government. These and other seasons of life impact the ways we shine. For a season, we must dream small, but we can fail to update our efforts to shine more radically when situations change. We are tempted to continue shining in the same way we did before we were freed from the temporary challenges. Even after we get a new job or are healed from our sickness, we may not adjust the energy and intentionality that we give to shining. As a result, a basket lowers over our lamp. Doing your best will not look the same in varying seasons. Stay alert and avoid getting stuck in outdated patterns that limit your shining.

2. Unable

Many people have pitiful views of themselves—especially regarding their usefulness to God. Many of us believe that we are too old, too young, too poor, or too something. We don't have the necessary education. We may feel that God did not give us the right personality to make a big impact on the world. Here's a news flash: God can and does use very old and very young people with any body type, with any bank balance, and with any Enneagram and Myers-Briggs personality type. A low and inaccurate view of your usefulness may be due to your own mistakes or the actions and words of others. The words "I can't" may also be an excuse for inaction. This is a common theme throughout history. Moses thought he was unqualified because of his lack of speaking ability, and Jeremiah thought he was too young. God knew better.

Even strong churches succumb to this underappreciation of what God can do. Decades ago, the leaders of Christ Church Memphis hesitated to affirm a long-term goal of its missions committee. They planned to train and equip ten families to relocate to an impoverished neighborhood in their city. The church leaders thought this community development strategy to bring light to a challenging and dark part of their city was unwise and impossible. But it happened. As of 2019, approximately four hundred people had moved into that neighborhood in order to bless the people and help restore jobs, security, and hope.[139]

God can and does use ordinary people and churches to do more than we imagine.

It can be difficult to silence the negative voices in your head, but one's confidence soars as she or he moves beyond the noise. After increasing numbers of adventurers attempted manned flight without success, the *Washington Post* declared, "It is a fact that man can't fly."[140] David McCullough describes the commitment of the Wright brothers in the face of such opposition. "In no way did any of this discourage or deter Wilbur and Orville, any more than the fact that they had had no college education, no formal technical training, no experience working with anyone other than themselves, no friends in high places, no financial backers, no government subsidies, and little money of their own. Or the entirely real possibility that … they could be killed."[141] To all of us who sometimes doubt our usefulness to God, Paul said, "I can do all things through God who strengthens me" (Philippians 4:13). Affirm your potential in God's hands and refuse the unable basket that would greatly hinder the impact of your shining.

3. Unworthy

Whereas the unable basket is related to one's abilities, this basket is related to one's being and core identity. There is a scene in the movie *Finding Neverland* that reminds me of our value and identity in Christ. Replying to a comment that his dog Porthos is "just a dog," the character Barrie replies, "Just a dog? Just? Porthos, don't listen. Porthos dreams of being a bear, and you want to shatter those dreams by saying he's just a dog? What a horrible candle-snuffing word. That's like saying, 'He can't climb that mountain, he's just a man,' or 'That's not a diamond, it's just a rock.'"[142]

I have heard negative, candle-snuffing voices about my own unworthiness: "I am not good enough. I am too broken. There are many people better suited for the mission." All of that is true, but God has a long history of using cracked pots like us to change the world. After affirming that God has made light shine in our hearts, Paul adds, "But we have this treasure in jars of clay to show that this all-surpassing power is from God and not from us" (2 Corinthians 4:6–7). You are the child of God. You are the light of the world. Remembering who you are in Christ will prevent the unworthy basket from limiting the way you shine.

4. Uncalled

I have rarely heard someone say "it's not my job" when asked about his or her role in God's mission, but it seems that many hold this view. One person says, "I don't have that gift." Another seeks to justify their lack of missions involvement by pointing out that their church does great things in outreach—made possible by their donations. Many people are confused about the whole idea of calling. Some Christians have a vocational calling to serve in mission and ministry. In many cases, these people are compensated for their ministry and receive little or no other income. In addition to the vocational calling that some receive, there is a general calling that everyone receives. Jesus calls Christians in every vocation and walk of life to serve in God's mission of light—including doctors, students, bankers, farmers, and retirees. This is part of the meaning of baptism. Interestingly, if you notice the vocations of the first twelve disciples, it seems that Jesus takes joy in using folks who are not ministry professionals. Right now is a good time to reaffirm your calling. Say these words out loud: "I am called to shine." By repeating these words and celebrating your calling, you can refuse this common basket. Shining God's love is indeed your job.

5. Unwilling

I may agree that I am called and recognize that I have certain gifts and abilities, but there is still one vital question. Am I willing to pay the price? God never said that this journey of discipleship would be easy. It takes sweat to run the race with excellence (1 Corinthians 9:24–27). Some people balk at the calling of God as they consider the possible changes that obedience might make on their own life plans.

For months, my Chinese friend Xu had been polite but resistant about the idea of following Jesus. Finally, he shared the reason: "I'm afraid of what God will ask of me." Does that sound familiar? When Jesus invites us to follow him, he presents us with a blank contract. Our signature communicates our willingness to do whatever God calls us to do. That is a bit scary, but God is good. Jesus said, "Whoever wants to be my disciple must deny themselves and take up their cross and follow me" (Matthew 16:24). Many complain silently, "It is hard enough trying to be light in our own families and communities. It is too hard to serve others. I just can't." That is a long way of saying, "I won't." The basket of unwillingness is so opaque that it can almost snuff out the flame of one's lamp.

6. Oblivious

All Christ followers love worship, Bible study, and gracious Christian fellowship. These are all good practices that build our faith and prepare us to serve. But remember my description of spiritually fat Christians. We can be so focused on our own blessings that we are unaware of the needs around us and on the other side of the world. I once saw a picture of this on a busy street in Orlando. I was driving in the fast lane, but the car in front of me was in no hurry, going well under the speed limit. I inched closer to the rear bumper of the slowpoke, hoping to encourage the car to speed up or move over. Finally there was an opportunity for me to pass in the right lane, and I darted over. As I passed by the slower car, I noticed the driver. She was enjoying her drive and seemed to be totally unaware of me or anyone else. She was smiling and singing with one hand lifted high. She was worshipping. She was caught up in the goodness of God. This is a snapshot of a common basket that afflicts Christ followers. We can be so enthralled with our experience with God's goodness that we ignore the urgent needs of others. We praise God, but we forget our equally important calling to remember and serve lost and hurting people. We fail to balance worship with witness as is the nature of cruciform discipleship. This oblivious basket looks holy, but it causes us to ignore our calling to shine.

7. Divided

Not all of the Israelites in the Exodus had single-hearted loyalty to God. Some flagrantly bowed down to images made of wood or gold, and others espoused a faith in Yahweh but held other priorities (gods) in their hearts. Likewise, it is easy for us to value some things on a level equal to or higher than the priority we give God. The Bible has a word for this: "idolatry." Anything, even something good and beautiful, that usurps allegiance due to God alone, is an idol. This broader understanding of idolatry is as common in America as it is anywhere else. Perhaps no baskets threaten our shining today more than materialism, an unbalanced focus on family, and a passion to create a sense of physical and financial security. Introducing his book *Untamed: Reactivating a Missional Form of Discipleship*, Allan Hirsch wrote, "Certain things, ideas, and relationships intrude themselves into the God-relationship and block our capacity to be all that Jesus intended us to be." Hirsch goes on, "Identifying these hindrances, and moving beyond them, opens us up to becoming impactful followers of Jesus."[143] God is a jealous for our single-hearted loyalty. God alone is worthy of worship, and the mission of light is crippled by idolatry.

8. Too Spiritual

More than a few people believe that making a strategy to shine is too businesslike and unspiritual. Reading the Bible and praying are nice "spiritual" undertakings but creating a plan to help others read the Bible and pray for the first time is too … something. I have tried to understand this reasoning, but it honestly sounds like an excuse for maintaining a low light. Consider the amount of planning and effort people put into selecting a new car, a school for their children, or a marketing plan for their company. Advancing the kingdom of God and serving the needs of the world are worth at least as much effort. A failure to think strategically about how we participate in God's light mission may demonstrate an underappreciation of our calling and the urgency of the world's needs. When we truly value something, we feel fine about spending resources to bring excellence. Is there anything more spiritual than asking God to help you develop plans to lift your lantern high?

9. Poisoned

I don't respond well to pushy salesclerks. When I encounter one, I find a way to communicate that his or her approach is not going to be effective with me. Some people are passionate about the specific missions they support. That's good, but unsensitive zeal often poisons the hearts of friends and family. We may turn a cold shoulder to the zealot ranting about his or her pet project, but we may also allow that extreme person or group to block the way we hear all invitations to participate in God's mission. Don't let the obnoxious behavior of well-meaning ministry zealots become a basket that limits the light cast by your lantern. Ignore the zealot and listen to Jesus's invitation to shine.

10. Comfortable

Some people routinely use the words "But we never did it that way before." These benevolent folks find it hard to develop high, excellent, and effective lanterns because that would involve change. If we keep learning, however, we will keep changing. There is a direct connection between our knowledge and our shining. If I have never heard of the needs of a certain group, why would I pray for them or consider ways to meet their needs? To consistently shine brightly, we must make the effort to keep learning and refuse another common saying: "Don't confuse me with the facts." With so much of our world in flux, rethinking and relearning have become as important as thinking and learning. Adam Grant, author of *Think Again: The Power of Knowing What You Don't Know*, recognizes this pattern as cognitive laziness. "We often prefer the ease of hanging on to old views over the difficulty of grappling with new ones."[144] It is easy to grow comfortable with our methods and areas of focus. This gives us a false sense of control even if the methods are not as effective as they may have been and the areas of greatest need are no longer the areas where we have focused. The strategic refuse to get too comfortable. Strategic Christians keep shining brightly by continuing to learn, analyzing their effectiveness, listening to God, and being open to change.

11. Nearsighted

Overwhelmed by the urgent needs around the world, some Christ followers become farsighted and ignore needs in their own communities. Even more folks are nearsighted. They tend to say things like "Once we meet the needs in our community, we can worry about the rest of the world." It is kind of a bloom-where-you-are-planted strategy. I understand the concern, but this statement is a half-truth. This philosophy of sequential impact is shaky at best. When would any Christian or church ever finish meeting local needs? If everyone waited on that to happen, the gospel would have never moved beyond Jerusalem. Acts 1:8 is clear about the geography of our mandate. Yes, we start our ministry in Jerusalem (our local culture), but we don't stop there. This nearsighted basket is well-known and quite a crowd pleaser, but it will strangle off light that could shine far beyond your house, neighborhood, ethnic group, and nation. Those who lack the ability to go to distant communities can shine God's love abroad through prayer, computer-based ministries, or by supporting others with finances. Take a moment to thank God for those pioneers who first brought the good news to your area. They refused to allow this basket to limit their impact.

12. Shortsighted

It is easy to be satisfied with benevolence—saving a few starfish—although additional research and effort might produce a more profound and lasting impact. In a bold essay in the early days of Nazi Germany, Dietrich Bonhoeffer outlined ways the German church might respond to suffering and injustice. He called Christians "not just to bandage the victims under the wheel, but to put a spoke in the wheel itself."[145] Although violence was part of Bonhoeffer's response in that historical setting, I include his words here to encourage Christ followers to think carefully about causes and cures for the pains and needs we seek to address. A commitment to address root causes of suffering can be costly, but strategic Christians courageously consider all options. An unemployed widow with young children has many needs, but a job training program with childcare would get her started toward independent living. A homeless man has many needs, but he can't land a job until he gets a picture ID. And the overarching cure for alienation, hopelessness, fear, and shame is a saving relationship with Jesus. Graciously meeting immediate needs is important (food, shelter, medical care), but the strategic also consider root causes and long-term solutions. To reject this shortsighted basket and shine brightly, think deeply about each need.

13. Independent

Although no local church is perfect, the community of faith continues to be the main instrument through which God communicates grace to the world. There will always be opportunities for us to shine as individuals, but we are designed to shine in community. A healthy and biblical rhythm of life includes gathering and scattering. We gather with other believers to remember and experience Christ. We participate in the sacraments, we confess our sins and brokenness, we affirm our faith, we worship, and then we send each other out as the light of the world. A solo lantern can make a difference, but participation with the Body of Christ multiplies the impact. We need each other. We need the prayers, encouragement, and accountability that participation in a team provides. "Let us consider how we may spur one another on toward love and good deeds, not giving up meeting together, as some are in the habit of doing, but encouraging one another" (Hebrews 10:24–25). Be a part of a community and refuse the independent basket.

14. Acclimated

One of the most amazing things about the human eye is its ability to help us see in bright sunlight as well as in near total darkness. It happened to me again yesterday as I sat down on my patio to read in the late afternoon. An hour later, my wife asked, "How can you read in the darkness?" Only when I looked up did I discover how dark it was. My eyes had become used to the darkness. At our home in Shanghai, I was surrounded by 30 million people. I was with these people every day in subways, markets, and on bustling sidewalks. Each of my neighbors was created in God's image, but I often forgot that most of them walk in spiritual darkness. Researchers say that only 5 percent are Christ followers and fewer than 50 percent have any accurate knowledge of the good news. My spiritual eyes sometimes get acclimated to the darkness.

Do you have a safe and comfortable place to live? Do you have access to health care? Do you feel relatively secure when you lock your doors? Are most of your friends Christians and do you enjoy fellowship often? Are you encouraged by Christian music, apps, books, and other sources of teaching and inspiration? Do you have any money in a bank account? I hope all of that and more is true for you. Our challenge is to not let our blessings lull us into a place where we forget that not everyone has these blessings. The basket of acclimation is slowly lowered, but the impact is significant.

15. Blind

People of all races and nationalities have the tendency to unjustly and unlovingly categorize and demean those they see as different. Like you, I've been greatly influenced by the various cultures in which I have lived. I learned many beautiful and helpful attitudes and traditions during my childhood in Mississippi. I was also impacted with ideas that are dark and destructive. Although many things in my life changed radically and quickly after my Christian conversion at age seventeen, my brokenness and blindness in the area of racial equality went mostly unrecognized and unchallenged for years. I did not act out in racist ways, and I was rarely aware that I had racist thoughts. Eventually, however, God helped me discover that I sometimes viewed people of color differently than I viewed people who had skin like mine.

Books like John Perkins's *Let Justice Roll Down: John Perkins Tells His Own Story* helped me better see the reality of racism in the world, in my background, and in my life.[146] My ongoing journey of healing and repentance has been encouraged by Bible study, prayer, and conferences, but relationships are the dominant tools God uses to free me from the light-blocking basket of racism. I'm eternally thankful for the influence of Memphis friends like Roy "Soup" Campbell and Eloise Mays, one black and one white. God also greatly used my relationships with people in cultures far beyond the white churches and neighborhoods of Mississippi and Tennessee to significantly impact the way I see and appreciate the beautiful diversity in God's children. Although the racism that most impacted me was a black and white divide, any bias based on skin pigmentation or ethnic background is a dark and deadly basket. It is impossible to have maximum impact on the world without confronting this blindness and beginning a journey of healing.

Moving Forward

The baskets that block your lamp will change from time to time, but they will keep coming. Distractions and temptations are a part of life. One of our ongoing challenges is to remember that God can use anyone. Any lantern, regardless of age, health, wealth, or education, can bring life-changing light. It is amazing what God can do when people courageously and intentionally lift their lanterns high and refuse to let baskets hinder their shining.

> ➤ David and Peggy were in their late seventies when they came to China to lift up Christ's light as teachers. No other teachers in their school were anywhere near their age. None made more impact than this patient, courageous couple that daily lifted their lanterns high with joy and excellence.

> When I met Emma, she was eight years old, and she had been praying for China every night since she was five. No one in her family had been to China. There were no Chinese children in her small community. She didn't know of any families who had adopted a child from China. There was no human explanation of why Emma had been praying for China. I was further amazed when she told me, "Someday I will go to China and tell them how much God loves them." Her witness spurred FollowOne International to launch a program that allowed children like Emma to do the things they are uniquely positioned to do in ministry: pray with faith and allow God to speak through their relationships with friends. Friends4One was a twenty-first century pen pal ministry that connected American kids with Chinese kids. Emma helped over one thousand American children lift their lanterns far higher than they or their parents imagined possible.

> After an error in surgery had made her a paraplegic, Nancy kept asking her friend Margaret, "Why is God keeping me here?" Margaret listened and prayed often with her, and they finally came up with an idea. Although her hands and arms had limited function, Nancy found a way to use her cell phone to call people who God put on her heart. The calls usually began with "Hi. This is Nancy. I'm just calling to check in on you. How are you doing, and how can I pray for you?" Nancy continued her gracious ministry as long as her wounded body allowed.

You are not unlike David, Peggy, Emma, and Nancy. You are busy and prone to distraction. You have limits. You are broken, fallible, mortal, and sinful. Your thinking is often flawed. But you are one for whom the Son of God died. You are filled with the Spirit. You are called to join God's mission of light, and God can use you.

I have been a basket case many times in my life. As I yield to self-pity, pride, or fear, I am prone to still allow baskets into my life. If you recognize one or more of the baskets I listed, don't panic or despair. I have good news. God is moving toward you even as you read. God is happy to restore a correct attitude about being the light of the world.

Your best response is to agree with the Spirit and ask God to help you change, to repent. As you move forward, keep listening to the Spirit and get the support of Christian friends when you realize flawed thinking is limiting your shining. At times you may need to shout, "Get that basket out of my life." No basket is too heavy for the Holy Spirit to lift. Getting rid of light-blocking baskets will release more light and love into the world for God's glory. This type of shining will bring you more peace, fulfillment, and joy, and you will make Jesus smile.

Be the Change

CHAPTER 14: BASKET CASES

Consider

- ➤ Was there a time in your life when you were shining more or less brightly than you are today?
- ➤ What might be the reasons for the fluctuation?

Interact

- ➤ Share which basket is a regular visitor to your lamp.
- ➤ Help each other consider possible ways to overcome those baskets and shine more brightly.

Pray

- ➤ Give thanks that God's grace shines brightly without limitation every day.
- ➤ Ask the Spirit to alert and guide you when a basket begins to diminish your shining.

- Pray for Christ followers who are shining brightly although they are experiencing difficult challenges in this season of their lives.

Act

- Choose one basket that is hoisted over your lamp. What is one thing you can do this week to cast off that distraction, shine brightly, and make Jesus smile?

Section III
MAXIMUM LIGHT

CHAPTER 15

Lantern Maintenance

So he said to me, "This is the word of the LORD to Zerubbabel: 'Not by might nor by power, but by my Spirit,' says the LORD Almighty."

—Zechariah 4:6

Highlights

> Even when we have a wonderful plan to shine brightly, poor daily lantern maintenance will result in dim days.

> To stay bright, we must keep a realistic and humble perspective as we focus on shining one day at a time.

> While the previous chapter offered ways to remove baskets that hinder your light, this chapter shares practices that stir up the flame of God in your life so you will shine all the brighter.

As a Christ follower, you are the light of the world. Nothing can change that reality. There are, however, factors within and around us that influence how we shine. The last chapter alerted you to some baskets that will limit the impact of your shining. In this chapter, you will find ways to maintain the brightness that the Spirit's presence gives to our lives.

It is one thing to acknowledge problems, inadequacies, or pain in our lives. It is something quite different to take steps to correct such issues. One day, my dog Sully was sleeping soundly at my feet as I read. Every few minutes he would yelp and twitch without opening his eyes. When I finally got up to leave the room, Sully jumped to his feet to follow me. Only then did I realize that he had been sleeping on top of a large wire brush I had left on the floor. The brush hurt too much for Sully to sleep soundly, but not enough for him to get up and move.

I hope this book does more than make you uncomfortable. I pray that God moves you to action. Even when you have a strategic plan to lift your lantern high, your light can lose its brilliance in the wear and tear of life. A lamp must be maintained in order to continue shining brightly.

The Wick

Think about these three aspects of a common lantern or lamp: the wick, the lens, and the flame. The condition of the wick determines the efficiency of the lamp. A wick that is too long will produce carbon, the waxy black muck that gets on the lantern lens, the walls, and the ceiling. The ideal length of a typical candle wick is one-eighth of an inch. This length helps ensure a clean burn with little smoke and maximum light. In the Jewish temple era, the priests were in charge of lighting and maintaining the lamps. One of their main responsibilities was trimming the wicks.

Your flame may have burned brightly in the past, but you may realize that something has changed about your brightness. It is easy to begin counting on past experiences to provide light for current opportunities. Perhaps your wick needs to be trimmed. Perhaps your faith needs to be updated, restated, or renewed. If you feel that your wick is barely glowing, invite the great high priest Jesus to trim your wick. God is in the transformation business. The Spirit will never leave, forsake, or ignore a wick that wants to burn brightly again. "A bruised reed he will not break, and a smoldering wick he will not snuff out" (Isaiah 42:3, Matthew 12:20). If you invite him, Jesus will keep your faith fresh and bright.

The Lens

The glass lens of a lantern must be clear and translucent for the flame to provide the maximum amount of light. The realities of life, however, tend to create smudges and dusty spots on the lenses of our lives. Habits, sins, unresolved issues, pains, or mis-aligned priorities can limit the brightness of our spiritual lanterns. Your wick may be burning with real faith, but your light will never be bright if the clarity of the lens is not maintained. C. S. Lewis's reference to dusty mirrors is a similar reminder: "[God] shows much more of Himself to some people than to others … not because He has favourites, but because it is impossible for Him to show Himself to a man whose whole mind and character are in the wrong condition. Just as sunlight, though it has no favourites, cannot be reflected in a dusty mirror as clearly as in a clean one."[147] It takes discipline to keep your lens clean.

The Flame

When Jesus referred to his first followers as the light of the world, these disciples had already expressed faith in Christ. They had yielded their hearts to the Light of the world. They had been set on fire and had begun the task of setting the world ablaze with God's love. Everything about a lamp can be excellent, but if there is no fire, there is no light. The first step in becoming a light that shines far is to allow God to set you on fire. The wick of our lives receives the Flame when we respond to God's grace with a prayer of gratitude, faith, and commitment to serve the purposes of Jesus. If you have made that commitment, be certain of this: God's Spirit abides in you. You are the light of the world. You have been set on fire.

Maintaining the Lantern

Shining brightly for Jesus every day takes intentionality and hard work. If you regularly follow these maintenance practices, your wick will stay trimmed, your lens will be clean, and the flame of God's presence will be fanned into brilliance.

1. Get free

I imagine that Lazarus walked out of his tomb smiling. He was glad to be alive although he was still bound in the clothes of death and darkness (John 11:43–44). Jesus brought Lazarus back to life, but others were enlisted to remove the grave clothes so he could be completely free. Hands that are bound with issues from one's past cannot lift a lantern as high as hands that are free. An unresolved pain, a broken relationship, a crippling fear, or a pattern of unfaithful behavior will hold us back from our potential. These grave clothes keep us from running freely, and they dim our light like soot on the lens of a lantern. In his book *Breathing Under Water: Spirituality and the Twelve Steps*, Richard Rohr explores the meaning of freedom. In a chapter entitled, "A Good Lamp," Rohr acknowledges that the truth will set us free (John 8:32), but he adds: "First it tends to make you miserable."[148] Although you are thankful to be in God's family, perhaps you are painfully aware that something is holding you back. Some pains will not just go away with time. Jesus can "set the oppressed free" (Luke 4:18), but we need to acknowledge the things that bind us. We need to tell God—and perhaps others—that we need help. You may want to shine brightly, but like Moses, before God can do a great work through you, the Lord may need to do more work in you. Take steps to deal with your brokenness. Talk honestly with a counselor, pastor, support group, or trusted friend. Jesus will set you free one day at a time.

2. Worship fully

Think back to one of the best worship services you ever experienced. Effective worship services inspire us, move us to praise God, inform us, encourage us, comfort us, bring healing, and woo us to repentance. But excellent worship should also move worshippers to action. Anything that draws us closer to Jesus should also draw us closer to his mission to lost and hurting people. Develop the habit of asking yourself these questions as you leave a worship service: "In response to what I heard and experienced, how should I live this week? What new ideas do I have about blessing others near and far?" Notice the connection between praising God and serving God's mission in passages like Hebrews 13:15–16: "Let us continually offer to God a sacrifice of praise—the fruit of lips that openly profess his name. And do not forget to do good and to share with others, for with such sacrifices God is pleased." In cruciform worship, we celebrate God reaching down to us in grace, and we respond with confession, praise, allegiance, and a renewed commitment to participate in our mission of light with excellence and intentionality. I once heard a missionary with Frontiers describe her team's worship time in a very restrictive country: "Every morning, we came in like sleepy kittens and came out like lions." Regular participation in worship experiences that move you up in praise and out in mission will help you keep your light shining brightly.

3. Express gratitude

The more we express gratitude for God's blessings, the more likely we will be a blessing to others. Remember that God has never given you a single blessing just for your own sake. Every gift is intended to bless you and be used by you to bless others. The supreme way to be grateful is to use the gift to remind someone of God's love. Expressing gratitude to God is a powerful discipline that reminds us who we are and who God is. We are called to respond to God's grace like the leper Jesus healed in Matthew 8:3–4 (MSG): "Your cleansed and grateful life, not your words, will bear witness to what I have done." When we express gratitude to our fellow pilgrims on earth, we humbly acknowledge our limitations as we acknowledge their generosity toward us. An attitude of gratitude keeps our flame alive, and expressions of gratitude always put a spotlight on God's goodness.

4. See the bottom line

Our tendency in reading scripture is to focus on how God wants to bless us. This style of reading often leads us to overlook the fuller meaning of a passage. The Bible is a cruciform message. If we read only the promises and blessings, we miss the bigger picture. Missionary, strategist, and author Don Richardson (1935–2018) referred to the "top line" and "bottom line" of Scripture.[149] Genesis 12:1–3 is one of many passages where the vertical and horizontal parts of the message are obvious: "I will bless you [top line] and you will be a blessing [bottom line]." Psalm 67:1–2 is another example: "May God be gracious to us and bless us … That your ways may be known on earth, your salvation among all nations." Only a vampire would read the top line and skip the bottom line. To keep your lantern bright, read scripture carefully, the top and the bottom line.

5. Breathe deeply

The best way to encourage a faltering flame is to provide it with more air. Consider the importance of oxygen to our bodies. If we only take shallow breaths, our body will function. But if we want peak performance, we must breathe deeply. Whether you realize it or not, Jesus has taken up residence in your life. By cultivating a constant awareness of the presence of the Holy Spirit, the Breath of God, we find strength for every challenge. In Colossians 1:27 (J. B. Phillips), Paul reminds us, "And the secret is simply this: Christ in you! Yes, Christ in you bringing with him the hope of all glorious things to come." An awareness of the Spirit's presence in your life will help keep you fired up and shining brightly. Let the wind of the Spirit fill your soul every morning. Breathe deeply.

6. Pray fully

We often pray with the same bias with which we read the Bible and participate in worship. It is easy to focus on the needs of our families and friends while ignoring the needs of those beyond our close networks.

Consider the list of concerns you are likely to hear when a group of Christians pray together. Often each request includes the words "me," "my," and "our." This focus may be evidence of vampiristic faith that asks only, "What's in it for me?" Be intentional about how you pray and whom you include. Think outside your own circle. Review the day's news with missional eyes. Ask yourself, "What does this information suggest about how I can pray, give, or serve?" Use the Lord's Prayer and cruciform scripture passages to help you pray fully. For example, pray the words of Colossians 4:2-5. "Devote yourselves to prayer, being watchful and thankful. And pray for us, too, that God may open a door for our message so that we may proclaim the mystery of Christ, for which I am in chains. Pray that I may proclaim it clearly, as I should. Be wise in the way you act toward outsiders; make the most of every opportunity."

7. Be encouraged

Many of us are surrounded by pre-Christian people or believers who are mostly selfish or benevolent. That's fine, but be intentional about spending some time with other strategic Christ followers. Finding these folks may be difficult, but start in your own church. You might need to launch and lead a high-lights group for prayer and discussion about how to shine brightly. Look for authors and leaders that promote missional and strategic living. Some might even correspond with you. Try to attend conferences focused on shining. Be creative in finding ways to hang out with other lights lifted high. Your shining and theirs will be encouraged. "And let us consider how we may spur one another on toward love and good deeds, not giving up meeting together, as some are in the habit of doing, but encouraging one another—and all the more as you see the Day approaching" (Hebrews 10:24–25).

8. Listen up

Nothing encourages us to shine more than the actual act of sharing with and serving people in need. Be intentional. Spend time with people beyond your culture and comfort zone at least monthly. Listen to and learn from them. As you begin to understand more about their experiences in darkness and light, your commitment to be the light of the world will be affirmed. God uses our interaction with people from different backgrounds and perspectives to open our eyes to depths of truth we have only begun to fathom. For many years, I have regularly discussed life and faith with Chinese friends, Christians and pre-Christians. The Spirit always uses their insights and questions to help me grow in my faith. When you interact with people from different cultures and backgrounds, listen to them with the expectant attitude of Paul: "I long to see you so that I may impart to you some spiritual gift to make you strong—that is, that you and I may be mutually encouraged by each other's faith" (Romans 1:11–12). The joy you experience as you serve others will confirm what you know in your heart: You were created for this purpose. You were born to shine.

9. Lean wisely

In our attempt to be strategic, we must remember that human reasoning and hard work are not enough. Even the strongest and brightest life needs a place to lean. Israel chose foolishly and leaned on Egypt (Isaiah 36:6). Trusting in our own labors, strategies, and plans to shine brightly would be an equally bad choice. You are the light of the world, but you were in darkness until God ignited your life. The flame in any lantern is fragile. Even the best plans will fail if we succumb to the temptation to trust in our human ability. The Psalmist said it this way: "Do not put your trust in princes, in mortal men, who cannot save. When their spirit departs, they return to the ground: on that very day their plans come to nothing. Blessed is he whose help is the God of Jacob, whose hope is in the Lord his God" (Psalm 146:3–5).

We are the light of the world and God's mysterious method for transforming darkness, but we remain vulnerable to the root sin that nips at us throughout life. Even if we build a tall lampstand and live strategically, pride can block how we shine. To stay bright, we must keep a humble perspective. Even when we shine with excellence, we are doing no more than following in the steps of Jesus. We shine only because he shines in us. It is easy, however, to compare ourselves to others and come away thinking of ourselves more highly than we should.

This is one reason that persecuted Christ followers shine brightly. They are utterly dependent on God. They are realistic about who they are. They realize their vulnerability and fragility. They see that their best plans to shine achieve nothing unless miracles happen. They have experienced God's power and light even in their suffering. They walk by faith. They lean on Jesus, and their peaceful confidence in darkness causes the world to see the light of God's grace.

Pride and humility are issues of the heart and the head. When Mississippi bluesman Jimmy "Duck" Holmes was nominated for a 2021 Grammy, a CBS interviewer asked him, "If you win a Grammy, will it go to your head?" Duck responded, "My head is like a concrete floor, you can't swell it." And then Duck shared how his mental attitude keeps his heart humble: "When you got something that you can share that's an honor." It honors God when we share the gifts we have received. This is like the moon remembering its important role as a reflector but not the source of light. God made us and uses us to shine, but we are the "lesser light" (Genesis 1:16).

The vision of Zechariah echoes this truth: God is the source of all light. God used Zechariah to offer words of comfort, consolation, and encouragement to Zerubbabel and the remnant of Israel as they returned to Jerusalem. In chapter 4 of Zechariah, the prophet shares a vision that includes a candlestick and a bowl supplied with oil by olive trees on either side of the candlestick. The angel then tells Zechariah, "'Not by might nor by power, but by my Spirit,' says the LORD Almighty" (Zechariah 4:6). One commentary explains the angel's message to Zerubbabel this way: "As the lamps burned continually, supplied with oil from a source (the living olive trees) which man did not make, so Zerubbabel need not be disheartened because of his weakness; for as the work is one to be affected by the living Spirit of God, man's weakness is no obstacle, for God's might will perfect strength out of weakness" (Hosea 1:7; 2 Corinthians 12:10; Hebrews 11:34). The Zechariah text is a preamble to Jesus's statement that we are the light of the world.

Working hard to build a high-light strategy and dependence on

God's Spirit are not mutually exclusive. Extremes on either end of this continuum, however, can lead to disaster. For example, a student who prays fervently but doesn't study will rarely receive excellent grades. China missionary J. Hudson Taylor testified that he learned "how much easier it is to lean on an arm of flesh than on the Lord; but I have learned too how much less safe it is." Jesus said, "I am the vine; you are the branches. If a man remains in me and I in him, he will bear much fruit; apart from me you can do nothing" (John 5:5). Work hard and lean on Jesus to shine brightly.

If you regularly follow godly practices like these, your wick will stay trimmed, your lens clean, and the flame of God's presence brilliant. By God's grace, you can cast off all light-blocking baskets and maintain your lantern so you can shine brightly. You can joyfully participate in God's great purpose for your life, change the world, and bring glory to God. I see this intentionality and humility in the way a successful businessman described his life goal in a recent letter to me: "I am one imperfect man that is determined to spread love and change lives for the rest of his time on earth." With humility, all Christ followers can celebrate this truth: God is using us to change the world!

You have heard the invitation. You understand enough to know that as a child of God you are the light of the world. You also know that God has given you the option of deciding how far and how brightly your light will shine. What else do you need?

Be the Change

CHAPTER 15: LANTERN MAINTENANCE

Consider

> ➤ In what ways has the author made you uncomfortable about the way you are shining for Jesus?

> Is the degree of your discomfort and the appeal of Jesus intense enough for you to begin making some changes?

Interact

> Share which types of lantern maintenance are routine for you. Which type do you most need today?
> How can you help each other with lantern maintenance?

Pray

> Confess any tendencies to lean on your own strength. In what areas of your life, do you sometimes think you don't need God?
> Acknowledge the Spirit's presence in your life—convicting, assuring, guiding, and empowering you to shine brightly.
> Pray for those who have never been set on fire by the grace of God and for Christians who have no one near them to help them maintain their lanterns.

Act

> What is one new action step you can take this week to maintain the health and vibrance of your light? Make a plan to take that step and share your commitment with someone.

CHAPTER 16

A Light Prayer

But you are a chosen people, a royal priesthood, a holy nation, God's special possession, that you may declare the praises of him who called you out of darkness into his wonderful light.

—1 Peter 2:9

Highlights

> There is a way to avoid being overconfident in your ability to shine brightly in a dark world.

> God's invitation to lift your lantern high awaits your response.

> Here is a prayer to help you begin living and shining brighter than you have imagined.

There can be an enormous gap between confidence and overconfidence. A recent survey of American adults asked if they thought they could triumph in battle against various animals without using a weapon.[150] The animal that respondents felt most confident about conquering was the rat, 28%. Interesting. But an overconfident and delusional 6% felt that they could defeat a grizzly bear. You are planning to shine brightly, but your struggle is with the ferocious bears of darkness and selfishness. What is the difference between being confident and overconfident as the light of the world?

When Jesus came into the world, he continued doing what he always does. The Son of God brings glory to his Father. Jesus's prayer in the hours before the crucifixion indicates that he has sent us into the world with that same mission. Jesus thought of us as he prayed to Father God: "As you sent me into the world, I have sent them into the world" (John 17:18). We are the light of the world. We shine in partnership with Jesus so the world might be changed for God's glory. Faithful partners shine with intentionality, urgency, excellence, and humility. This chapter will help you take the key step that connects your desires, best plans, and hard work with God's power and grace. Your attitude about shining may be bold, but any confidence in lifting your lantern high in the face of bears like darkness and selfishness will be overconfidence. There is only one reason for confidence. Hold tightly to the hand of Jesus, the Lion of Judah.

Light Me Up

You may have been following Christ for decades or only a few days. You may have taken many sideroads and fallen often, or you may have moved steadily forward in faith. You may have shined well or not so much. You may have made great progress in building a taller lampstand or not even started. None of that matters at this moment. I invite you to take a few minutes to be honest with God about your calling to be the light of the world. Do you want to shine in a way that honors God and brings light to people near and far? This prayer can help you take the next step in your journey of light. Slowly pray the words aloud.

> Dear Father of Light,
> Thank you for creating light that we might see your creation and give you praise.
> Thank you for sending your Son into darkness to be our Savior, my Savior.
> Thank you for welcoming me into your family of light.
> I receive your words by faith and agree that I am the light of the world.

I confess, however, that my sins, brokenness, and laziness have hindered how I shine.

Forgive me. Heal me. Wipe away any impurities that dim my light.

Deliver me from any baskets that limit the way I shine for you.

Light me up with your Holy Spirit.

I want to shine brightly and far.

I want to honor you with excellence in my life. You deserve my best.

So many are languishing in darkness: alone, without hope, and unaware of your grace.

So many efforts to shine have little impact: never touching urgent needs or transforming lives.

Something needs to change. I need to change.

Help me to live, love, and give strategically so that many will taste your grace and respond in faith.

Lord, I want to be the change.

Use me in ways greater than I have imagined to change the world for your glory.

Amen.

You have traveled the Christian journey long enough to know that God is faithful. If you prayed the above prayer in faith and humility, the Lord heard you. God smiles at your desire to live a life that blesses your community and the world. Expect your prayer to be answered. It may or may not be obvious to you in this lifetime, but God will use you to change lives, to change the world, and to chase away darkness with the light of the gospel. The Spirit will give you guidance and power as you give your whole heart to God and your best effort to bless others. Your confidence is in Christ, the light of the world.

Raising Your Albedo

Metrics for determining how brightly we shine are limited, but science has ways to measure light. The word "lumen" is the standard term used to describe light output—the higher the number of lumens, the brighter the light. Lumens are to light what pounds are to potatoes or gallons are to gasoline. A candle gives off about 12 lumens, but a sixty-watt soft white incandescent lightbulb produces about 840 lumens. One of the brightest normal-use bulbs today produces 5,500 lumens. Good lighting enables people to see what they otherwise would not appreciate. Think of the careful lighting museums provide for masterpieces on display. Often you don't even see the light fixture; you see only what it highlights.

Think again about the moon. Scientists use the term "albedo" to describe how well an object in the solar system reflects light, ranging between 0 (dark) and 1 (bright).[151] When astronauts first walked on Earth's moon, they reported that the surface was dark gray, like the color of dried cement. Our moon reflects only about 12 percent of the sun's light that hits it, which gives the moon an albedo of 0.12. Saturn's moon, however, reflects a whopping 99 percent of the light that falls on it.[152]

Unlike moons, stars, lightbulbs, or lanterns, we humans make choices that help determine how much light shines from us. This book is a tool to help you raise your albedo. It offers a process for you to polish up and optimize your life in order that the maximum amount of God's light might reflect on others. A candle provides a small amount of light, but wouldn't you rather shine like the 5,500-lumen bulb? We appreciate the moonlight we see on Earth, but wouldn't you rather reflect God's light like Saturn's moon? The brighter we shine, the more people notice God's beauty and goodness.

Yes, You Can

This invitation to shine brightly is not given only to those rare Christian superstars on the level of Olympic athletes, summa cum laude graduates, or the Apostle Paul. The words of 2 Corinthians 3:18 and countless other texts extend the invitation to all who believe in Jesus. Strategic living and shining with excellence are possibilities for every Christ follower, even those who are in difficult situations. Carol Lee Hamrin and Stacey Bieler have written about the dominant role of ordinary Chinese Christians in the evangelization of China—often when missionaries or other ministers were not allowed or available. "Like light, they offered hope and truth to others in dark times of despair." The writers summarized the impact of these lanterns lifted high: "Their faith, a transcendent anchor for their souls, gave them the insight and courage to make a difference in their chosen professions."[153] God's light shining through common, ordinary people can transform lives and the world. All of us are called and equipped to shine brightly.

As you consider this invitation to live and shine strategically, you may be shaking your head and mumbling something about the complexity of your situation. You may be saying, "I get it, but James doesn't understand my life." You are correct. I don't understand, but Jesus does. Please hear the invitation again. God wants you to shine, created you to shine in ways that are right for you, and gave you the Holy Spirit to light you up.

Ever since humans began living on beautiful planet earth, we have looked up at night and wondered about the moon. Eventually, science fiction authors like Jules Verne and scientists like Wernher von Braun dreamed of space travel. But everything changed when Neil Armstrong stepped onto the lunar surface in 1969. Scientists around the world immediately began to work more diligently on space travel. The reason was more than competition. Once a pioneer pierces a barrier, others believe that they, too, might reach that goal. It no longer seems impossible. Much of our hesitation to push against a perceived limitation is erased as we think, "If he did it, maybe I can." This book is dedicated to all those who push forward in the face of countless obstacles to announce and exhibit the unconditional, transforming grace of Jesus Christ in new ways and in unreached areas. The world is a better place and God is glorified because of the sacrificial lives of saints like the Apostle Paul, Hudson Taylor, William Wilberforce, Amy Carmichael, Moses Xie, and Pauline Hord. In this invitation and guide to shining, I have introduced over forty individuals who have lifted their lanterns high for God's glory. My parade of high lights includes people old and young, with both significant formal education and hardly any, busy people and those tired and retired, and rich and poor people in several countries. Dear sister or brother, the glow from your lantern may not look much like the lamp of anyone I have mentioned in this book, but here is the gospel truth: you can shine brightly.

Dark times, Bright Opportunities

In the twists and turns of life, there will be many challenges and baskets that will seek to limit or even extinguish your light. Sometimes your lantern will seem insignificant, unwanted, unnecessary, or forgotten. It is my great honor to have been friends with some of the bold patriarchs of God's Church in China. I was introduced to Allen Yuan (Yuán Xiāngchén, 1914–2005) at a house church meeting in his small Beijing apartment in 1997. After the Communist revolution, Yuan was imprisoned for refusing to stop preaching. The harsh realities of his incarceration soon made him physically weak and almost blind, but Yuan did not focus on the things he could not do. As Norman H. Cliff writes of Yuan, "What he could do he did."[154] He found a way to shine. All of God's children can shine brightly.

Sometimes an opportunity to shine will be connected with a great joy in your life. Often, however, a unique opportunity to shine will come when life is dark and hope is hiding. At this moment, many Christians are walking in the deep darkness of hunger, war, persecution, and martyrdom. You may also be in a situation where shining for Jesus involves a great cost. This has often been the case for God's children of light. Speaking of the persecution by the Roman emperor Nero, Tacitus described how some Christians in Rome passed into glory: "Covered with the skins of beasts, they were torn by dogs and perished, or were nailed to crosses, or were doomed to the flames and burnt, to serve as a nightly illumination, when daylight had expired."[155] Instruments of darkness like Nero sometimes feel that they have the ability to snuff out the light, but they are wrong. Jesus rose from the dead, and in our own suffering and death, we too can rise and shine.

Especially in the hard times of life, our choice to shine can have a massive impact. Consider the witness of Mat and Cindy Lipscomb. Two of their three young daughters were among the casualties of a devastating train accident near Chicago in 1999. The accident immediately attracted media attention, and the Lipscombs were approached by CNN and other networks for permission to broadcast the funeral service for their daughters. Shocked but open to consider what some saw as an invasion of personal grief, Mat and Cindy asked me to pray with them about the request. As we prayed, one reality hit my mind: "The worship service honoring Rainey and Lacey might be the only good news some people will hear tomorrow." With joyous anticipation about how God would use the death of their daughters, the Lipscombs said yes to the media. Millions of viewers around the world experienced the memorial service. It was a tearful but joyous celebration that showed Christ followers grieving—but not as those without hope. The Lipscomb family and friends remembered their daughters and Jesus's resurrection in the certainty that light overcomes darkness. In the following days and years, Mat and Cindy went on to share about the sustaining love of Jesus on The Today Show, Good Morning America, and various other radio and television programs and national publications. Media analysts estimate that over 28 million people were exposed to God's light through their witness in the first two years after the tragedy.[156] I hope you will never experience this depth of darkness, but the heartaches and the joys of your life will give you a unique platform to shine. All things—even our pain—can be used to shine light on God's goodness.[157] The words of the Apostle Paul encourage us: "I eagerly expect and hope that I will in no way be ashamed, but will have sufficient courage so that now as always Christ will be exalted in my body, whether by life or by death. For to me, to live is Christ and to die is gain" (Philippians 1:20–22). Your expression of hope and God's sustaining love may be the only grace some people will hear. Ask God to prepare you to use whatever life brings to shine for Jesus.

Living with Confidence

Strategic living flows from an intentionality to be the best possible steward of God's blessings in order that the maximum number of lives are transformed and God is honored. A person who trusts in Jesus and lifts his or her lantern high will be:

> **Imperfect but empowered:** You will not be overconfident about shining, trusting in your hard work and detailed planning. You will be confident because of God's grace and God's promise to empower fallible people to change the world. You will remember that without Christ you can achieve nothing, and with Christ you cannot fail.
> **Gracious and joyful:** God's presence in you will give you a joy and passion for serving others that is so profound that people will be drawn to the Source of your peace and compassion. You will love others like God loves you.
> **Active and prayerful:** As a cruciform disciple, you will keep a healthy balance in how you listen and speak, pray and serve, plan and take action. Excellence will characterize the ways you pray and the ways you live out your faith.

This is a good time to recall your identity and rehearse your answer to the question, "Who are you?" Before you are a wife, son, employee, old man, senator, preacher, or any other title or position, you are the light of the world. You were born to shine. Reclaim that identity as you receive Peter's teaching in 1 Peter 2:9 regarding our role in God's mission of light. We are sanctified, anointed, royal, holy, and set apart for God's purposes. It is amazing how God is working through ordinary people like you and me to change lives and transform the world. Holding the powerful hand of Jesus, we shine in the darkness with confidence even as we look for that day when Light will come with glory to chase away all darkness forever.

Be the Change

CHAPTER 16: A LIGHT PRAYER

Consider

> ➤ Does the bright witness of friends and the language in this book frustrate you more than encourage you? Consider why that may be true.
> ➤ Name the bear in your life that creates fear about shining brightly?

Interact

> ➤ Discuss the traits that will characterize a Christ follower who begins to live strategically: imperfect but empowered, gracious and joyful, and active and prayerful.
> ➤ Which of those seems most important to you? Which is the least obvious in your life?

Pray

> ➤ Thank God for using this book to offer you an invitation to shine in new ways.
> ➤ Ask God to give you at least one more shining friend to walk with you as you live strategically.
> ➤ Pray for those who do not have access to clean water and for those who are working to bring water and Living Water to those who thirst.

Act

> ➤ Go outside (rain or shine). Tilt your head back and appreciate anew the light God has given you—the light of the sun and the light of the Son.
> ➤ With boldness and faith, ask God to light you up and help you be the light of the world.

CHAPTER 17

Victorious Light

There will be no more night. They will not need the light of a lamp or the light of the sun, for the Lord God will give them light. And they will reign for ever and ever.

—Revelation 22:5

Highlights

- › As we await the coming of Christ in victory, we continue to shine in ways that bring God glory and transform lives.
- › Our knowledge that Christ will return in bright victory provides hope and joy even when our shining seems inadequate for the darkness around us.
- › God is worthy of our highest praise for all eternity, and God is worthy of our most excellent service now.

You are the light of the world. You were born to shine. Not unlike the star over Bethlehem, you shine so that people notice, are drawn to, and worship the Savior—Christ, the Lord.

What are your thoughts and emotions when you look up at the stars? The recent pictures from NASA's James Webb Space Telescope took my breath away. Wherever I am in the world, I try to find my nighttime friends Jupiter, Saturn, and Mars. As I look at them and their companions, I am often moved to consider again the mystery and power of light and the greatness of our Creator. My interest in astronomy began in a unique way when I was eighteen years old. Billy and I had been following Jesus for one year, and we shared a desire to be all that God wanted us to be. That desire took us to Billy's remote cabin on Pelahatchie Lake for a spiritual retreat. Among other things, we wanted God to reveal more to us about the Holy Spirit. After spending time reading, praying, listening, and talking in the cabin, about midnight we went outside and sat on the pier. The night was dark, as clouds masked the light from the moon and stars. We sat in silence for several minutes, praying, thinking of the Bible verses we had read together, and waiting. We expected to hear from God, and after several minutes, we began to sense God's nearness. If we had been wearing shoes, we would have taken them off as the pier became a holy place.

At some point, Billy was reminded of the closing chapter of the Bible, and he read aloud: "There will be no more night. They will not need the light of a lamp or the light of the sun, for the Lord God will give them light. And they will reign for ever and ever" (Revelation 22:5). After we silently reflected on those words a few moments, something—or Someone—caused us to look up at the sky. In glorious shock, we saw that the dark night had been transformed. The clouds had passed, and we gazed at a bright moon and a billion stars. We worshipfully wept, laughed, and hugged. We interpreted this heavenly display as confirmation that God was present. We were assured that we were the children of God and sons of light.

Part of the Spirit's gift to us that night was a reminder that God does not forget us. When life is tough, when we are racked by pain, when we are floundering in indecision, and when the night is black, it is easy to feel that God is distant. Dark feelings sometimes mask the reality of God's presence and light. As we live in the epoch between the first and second comings of Jesus, there are times when darkness seems to have the upper hand. Although we work hard to lift our lanterns high, we may sometimes be tempted to sigh, "Why bother with shining when my light seems to be so inadequate for the profound darkness?" In those low moments, it is important to breathe in the Spirit and put your struggle in a much broader context.

The ultimate victory of light is certain. Someday, maybe soon, God will make all things right as light conquers darkness forever. The foreknowledge of this victory can provide hope and joy regardless of how dark our skies are today. Timothy Tennent, president of Asbury Theological Seminary, makes the connection between our struggle to shine now and the greater Light that is to come. "Missions must increasingly be seen as flowing forth from God's initiative to Abraham to bless all nations (Genesis 12:3) and moving toward that day in the New Creation when men and women 'from every nation, tribe, people and language' will be worshipping our Lord Jesus Christ" (Revelation 7:9).[158] With one eye we look at the challenge of darkness today, but our other eye is fixed on the eastern sky and the return of Christ. Wess Stafford writes about the glorious day when he will run into the arms of Jesus: "He will reach down to wipe away my tears, but I pray that he also has to wipe the sweat off my brow."[159] As we await the coming of Christ in victory, we continue to shine in ways that bring God glory and transform lives.

In chapter nine, I introduced Pauline Hord, the amazing woman who used a ministry of prayer and education to shine brightly for Jesus. In 2003, Miss Pauline (at age ninety-six) reminisced with me about some of the letters she received from prisoners around the world. After recalling several, she hesitated, smiled broadly, and whispered one word: "Heaven." For several minutes, she shared longingly about the coming day when she would walk with Jesus and he would talk to her about the stars and the flowers and love. I took her wrinkled beautiful hand and added, "And my sister, there will be thousands of people there to greet you, those who experienced the grace of God because you served them with excellence and grace." With sparkling eyes, she replied, "That will be a glorious reunion. It will be wonderful. I can't believe it."[160] And then she laughed and laughed with the joy of one who would soon hear the words "Well done, good and faithful servant" (Matthew 25:21). A bright light. A lantern lifted high. Pauline Hord's life is an example, and this book is your invitation.

God has chosen to give us few details regarding the coming victory of light or the nature of heaven, but one thing is certain: heaven involves light. Near the end of William P. Young's book *The Shack*, the main character is given a peek into the reality of heaven. The book is Christian fiction, but the images build my faith in the Lord of light. From an elevated position, the main human character, Mack, looks across a meadow and sees countless children, small points of light, emerging from the forest. They glow not because they hold candles or lanterns; they themselves are lights. As they circle up and hold hands, a group of larger lights encircles them—adults. Beyond these two glowing circles are the angels, who appear as even taller flames of light. With all the points of light in place, the celebration continues. "A hush descended. The anticipation was palpable. Suddenly, to their right and from out of the darkness emerged Jesus, and pandemonium broke out. He was dressed in a simple brilliant white garment and wore on his head a simple gold crown, but He was every inch the King of the universe ..."[161]

Jesus is the Light of the world. Someday we will see him in all his brilliant glory. In the meantime, we shine as the moon reflects light from the sun. That is what you were created to do. You were born to shine. Reclaim your identity as the light of the world. Lift your lantern high, and may a pandemonium of praise and singing break out as the world sees our good works and gives God the glory.

"Is He Worthy?" is a beautiful hymn on this theme. The poet asks questions like "Do you feel the world is broken?" "Do you feel the shadows deepen?" "Do you wish that you could see it all made new?" A question-and-answer rhythm calls listeners to remember the dark realities of today but to celebrate the sweet and certain promise for tomorrow.

Is a new creation coming?
It is.
Is the glory of the Lord to be the light within our midst?
It is.
Is it good that we remind ourselves of this?
It is.[162]

I pray that this book has reminded you that the glory of the Lord is in our midst and that you are the light of the world. In closing, I have two questions and an invitation for you:

Is God worthy of your highest praise for all eternity?

Is God worthy of your most excellent service now?

Reclaim your identity as the light of the world, and lift your lantern high as a gift to God! You were born to shine.

Be the Change

CHAPTER 17: VICTORIOUS LIGHT

Consider

> ➤ Think about heaven for a minute. How might the reality of this gift of God influence the way you shine?

Interact

> ➤ What is one struggle or pain in the world where it seems like darkness is winning?
> ➤ What is it about heaven that most encourages you and gives you hope?

Pray

> ➤ Thank God for heaven.
> ➤ Pray that the way you shine will be used to encourage many to respond in faith to the Lord of heaven and earth.
> ➤ Pray for those bright lights who are facing the end of their earthly lives and those who are serving them.

Act

> ➤ Review the parts of the book you have underlined or highlighted. Thank God for speaking to you.
> ➤ If you have not already completed a plan to build a taller lampstand, give yourself a deadline.
> ➤ Tell one person how God is using this book to help you shine more brightly than you have imagined.

About the Author

James Loftin is founder and president of FollowOne International (est. 2004), a mission that provides coaching and resources to help churches, organizations, and Christ followers have maximum impact on their communities and the world. Prior to FollowOne, James was dean of the chapel and director of missions at Asbury Theological Seminary (Orlando campus). He also served as the minister of missions in several churches and was a senior corporate consultant with Awake Consulting and Coaching. In addition to serving on the small team that started the Orlando Campus of Asbury Seminary, Reverend Loftin helped launch an international school in Asia and two nonprofit ministries in the US that continue to excel. Break Thru Ministries is a youth ministry based in Mississippi that offers year-round programs and involves thousands of teenagers and youth ministry workers from across the nation. Service Over Self (SOS) is an urban ministry in Tennessee that has repaired over eleven hundred homes at no cost to owners by utilizing donated supplies and over twenty-five thousand volunteers.

James holds an undergraduate degree in sociology from Mississippi State University and a master of divinity from Asbury Theological Seminary. He has listened, learned, and served in urban and rural settings in over forty nations. After living in China for five years, James and his wife, Vivien, came to the United States for a short vacation in early 2020. Unable to return to Asia due to the pandemic, the Loftins made a home in Georgia. James continues to serve in the ministry of FollowOne, and Vivien is an educator with a specialization in teaching English and Mandarin as a second language. They enjoy exploring nature, trying new foods, and making friends.

James loves to hear from people who want their lives, organizations, or churches to have maximum impact. If you want to provide feedback on the book or get help in creating a plan to shine more brightly, email the author or visit the website below.

info@followone.org
BornToShine.info

Notes

1   Christopher McDougall, *Born to Run: A Hidden Tribe, Super Athletes and the Greatest Race the World Has Never Seen* (New York: Alfred A. Knopf, 2009).

2   Watchman Nee, *The Normal Christian Life* (n.p.: Christian Literature Crusade, 2009).

3   Thomas Merton, *New Seeds of Contemplation* (New York: New Directions, reprint edition, 2007), chap. 5, Kindle.

4   For a list of statistics, see chapter 6 Light Mission Status.

5   This quote is often attributed to D. T. Niles (1908–1970), a prominent mission and evangelism leader from Sri Lanka. I did not, however, find documentation of Niles being the original source.

6   *Chariots of Fire*, directed by Hugh Hudson, released April 9, 1982, by Twentieth Century-Fox Film Corporation, Allied Stars Ltd., and Enigma Productions, starring Ben Cross, Ian Charleson, Ian Holm, Alice Krige, et al.

7   Charles John Ellicott, "Commentary on Matthew 5:15 in Ellicott's Commentary for English Readers," *Biblehub.com*, accessed January 4, 2021, https://www.biblehub.com/matthew/5-15.htm#commentary.

8   "Sophie Scholl Biography," *Biography Online*, accessed June 2, 2022, https://www.biographyonline.net/women/sophie-scholl.html.

9   Albert Barnes, "Commentary on Matthew 5:14," *Barnes' Notes on the Whole Bible*, accessed May 9, 2020, https://biblehub.com/commentaries/barnes/matthew/5.htm.

10 The origin of "This Little Light of Mine" is uncertain. Some have reported that it was written in the 1920s by Harry Dixon Loes, but Wikipedia states that Loes "never claimed credit for the original version of the song, and the Moody Bible Institute where he worked said he did not write it." John Lomax and Alan Lomax made the earliest known recording of the song in 1934 (https://en.wikipedia.org/wiki/This_Little_Light_of_Mine).

11 Starthrower Foundation, "The Star Thrower Story," accessed November 22, 2020, https://starthrowerfoundation.org/.

12 *Ibid*.

13 Flourishanyway, "71 Songs About Changing the World," *Spinditty*, September 9, 2020, accessed December 10, 2020, https://spinditty.com/playlists/Songs-About-Changing-the-World.

14 Anastasia Tsioulcas, "10 Songs That Rallied Resistance Around the World," *NPR Music*, December 11, 2019, accessed January 9, 2020, https://www.npr.org/2019/12/11/778227017/10-songs-that-rallied-resistance-around-the-world.

15 Auguste Comte, *The Works of Auguste Comte: System of Positive Polity or Treatise on Sociology*, vol. 1 (n.p.: Editions Anthropos, 2007), 7–10.

16 Oswald Chambers, *My Utmost for His Highest*, "May 15" (n.p.: Discovery House, 2010), Kindle.

17 Tony Lambert, "The One-Legged Scotsman Who Sparked a Mission Movement in China," *OMF*, April 5, 2018, accessed February 5, 2020, https://omf.org/us/one-legged-scotsman-mission-movement-china/.

18 James Taylor, interviewed by Malcolm Gladwell, "James Taylor Comes Clean," *Broken Record,* 2020, podcast audio, accessed March 15, 2021, https://brokenrecordpodcast.com/episode-36-james-taylor-comes-clean/.

19 "Light," *Merriam-Webster.com*, accessed April 8, 2019, https://www.merriam-webster.com/dictionary/light.

20 William Harris and Craig Freudenrich, "How Light Works," *HowStuffWorks.com*, July 10, 2000, accessed December 1, 2020, https://science.howstuffworks.com/light.htm.

21 "What Is Light—An Overview of the Properties of Light," *Andor*, accessed November 5, 2020. http://www.andor.com/learning-academy/what-is-light-an-overview-of-the-properties-of-light.

22 Dr. Gary Zank, email to C. Ray Hayes on March 1, 2020. Dr. Zank's titles and positions at the University of Alabama in Huntsville include eminent scholar and distinguished professor, director of the Center for Space Plasma and Aeronomic Research, chair of the Department of Space Science, trustee professor, and fellow of the US National Academy of Sciences.

23 Kelly Tatera, "Isolation in the Dark Drives Humans to Brink of Insanity, Studies Find," *The Science Explorer*, November 19, 2015, accessed November 5, 2020, http://thescienceexplorer.com/brain-and-body/isolation-dark-drives-humans-brink-insanity-studies-find.

24 1 Kings 8:12; Psalm 97:2.

25 2 Samuel 22:29; Job 5:14; 3:4–6; 18:6; Psalm 107:10; Proverbs 20:20; Isaiah 8:22, 9:2; Ezekiel 30:18; 2 Peter 1:19.

26 Job 19:8; Isaiah 9:2, 60:2; Matthew 6:23; John 1:5; 3:19; 1 John 2:11.

27 Psalm 82:5; Proverbs 2:13–14; John 3:19; Romans 13:12; Ephesians 5:11; 1 Thessalonians 5:4–7.

28 1 Samuel 2:9; Job 10:21; 17:13; Psalm 88:12; Ecclesiastes 11:8.

29 Matthew 16:27, Psalm 107:10, Exodus 10:21; Lamentations 3:2; Ezekiel 32:8; Matthew 8:12; 25:30.

30 My eye doctor told me the injury to my eye was irreversible. God had other ideas. After I had worn a patch for six months, he examined me one last time. I had regained about 80 percent of my vision and was able to wear contact lenses again—an ability that was supposedly impossible because of the scar tissue. Thank you, Jesus.

31 Helen Keller, *The Story of My Life: with Her Letters (1887–1901) and a Supplementary Account* (n.p.: Digireads.com, 2017), chap. 4, Kindle.

32 National Aeronautics and Space Administration, "The Sun and Us," accessed March 1, 2021, https://history.nasa.gov/EP-177/ch3-1.html.

33 Gregg Okesson, *A Public Missiology: How Local Churches Witness to a Complex World* (Grand Rapids: Baker Academic, 2020), 7.

34 Cory Asbury, vocal performance of "Reckless Love," by Caleb Culver, Cory Asbury, and Ran Jackson, released October 27, 2017, on album *Reckless Love* by Bethel Music.

35 "Stories of Sacrifice: Desmond T. Doss," *Congressional Medal of Honor Society*, accessed August 22, 2019, https://www.cmohs.org/recipients/desmond-t-doss.

36 Rebecca Hawkes, "Hacksaw Ridge: the Extraordinary True Story of Desmond Doss, the War Hero Who Refused to Kill," the *Telegraph*, January 25, 2017, accessed June 1, 2020, https://www.telegraph.co.uk/films/0/mel-gibsons-hacksaw-ridge-the-extraordinary-true-story-of-desmon/.

37 Paul Baloche, "Open the Eyes of My Heart, Lord," *Integrity's Hosanna! Music (ASCAP)*, admin. CapitolCMGPublishing.com, 1997.

38 Bishop Christopher Wordsworth, quoted by Charles John Ellicott, "Commentary on James 1:17," in *Ellicott's Commentary for English Readers*, 1905, accessed November 4, 2019, https://www.studylight.org/commentaries/ebc/james-1.html.

39 Lesslie Newbigin, *The Household of God: Lectures on the Nature of the Church* (1953; repr., Eugene, Oregon: Wipf & Stock, 2008), 27.

40 Warren Cole Smith and John Stonestreet, *Restoring All Things: God's Audacious Plan to Change the World Through Everyday People* (Grand Rapids: Baker Books, 2015).

41 Irenaeus, *Against Heresies*, V:16, cited in Thomas C. Oden, *Classic Christianity: A Systematic Theology* (New York: Harper Collins, 2009), 66.

42 William T. Cavanaugh, "I had to learn to love the church: Then I had to learn to love God," *Christian Century*, June 7, 2021, accessed November 1, 2021, https://www.christiancentury.org/article/how-my-mind-has-changed/i-had-learn-love-church?fbclid=IwAR1cuoIIQ3m8Vjw6EzQ7vI9o44_3dMmQ.

43 George Scott Railton, *The Authoritative Life of General William Booth* (n. p.: Andrews UK Limited, 2012), chap. 3, Kindle.

44 "Bystander Effect," *Psychology Today*, accessed June 16, 2021, https://www. psychologytoday.com/us/basics/bystander-effect/.

45 "Bystander Intervention Training to Stop Anti-Asian/American and Xenophobic Harassment," *Hollaback!*, accessed March 23, 2021, https://www. ihollaback.org/bystanderintervention.

46 Martin Luther King Jr., "Martin Luther King Jr. Speech—January 1965 (Atlanta GA)," Nobel Prize Recognition Dinner at the Dinkler Plaza Hotel, January 14, 2019, accessed January 3, 2020, https://www.youtube.com/ watch?v=a_VxuOmxdsg.

47 J. Herbert Kane, *Wanted: World Christians* (Grand Rapids: Baker Book, 1986), 105.

48 Charles Van Engen, *God's Missionary People: Rethinking the Purpose of the Local Church* (Grand Rapids: Baker House 1991), 17.

49 Jürgen Moltmann, *The Church in the Power of the Spirit: A Contribution to Messianic Ecclesiology* (London: SCM, 1977), 64.

50 Gungor, vocal performance of "The People of God" written by Michael Gungor, Israel Houghton, and Brandon Gillies, released February 16, 2010 on album *Beautiful Things* by Brash Records.

51 Joseph H. Thayer, "STRONGS NT 649: ἀποστέλλω," *Thayer's Greek Lexicon*, 2011 by Biblesoft, Inc., accessed October 13, 2020, https://biblehub.com/ greek/649.htm.

52 "Barna Highlight: A Surprising Response to the 'Great Commission,'" email to author from the Barna Group, March 29, 2021, an excerpt from *Translating the Great Commission*, https://www.barna.com/.

53 Barna Group, "The Great Disconnect: Reclaiming the Heart of the Great Commission in Your Church," (n.p.: Barna, 2022), 17.

54 Keith Ferdinando, "Mission: A Problem of Definition," *Themelios* 33.1, no. 47 (2008), accessed March 2, 2020, https://www.thegospelcoalition.org/ themelios/article/mission-a-problem-of-definition/.

55 "Almost Half of Practicing Christian Millennials Say Evangelism Is Wrong," *Barna Group*, February 5, 2019, accessed July 2, 2020, https://www.barna. com/research/millennials-oppose-evangelism.

56 Christine Pohl, "Practicing Hospitality in the Face of 'Complicated Wickedness,'" *Wesleyan Theological Journal* 42, no. 1 (Spring 2007), 11.

57 Gregg Okesson, *A Public Missiology: How Local Churches Witness to a Complex World* (Grand Rapids: Baker Academic, 2020), 3.

58 "Integral Mission," Lausanne Movement, accessed November 22, 2020, https://lausanne.org/networks/issues/integral-mission.

59 Ray Bakke, *A Theology as Big as the City* (Downers Grove: IVP Academic, 1997), 34.

60 David C. Kirkpatrick, "Died: C. René Padilla, Father of Integral Mission," *Christianity Today*, April 27, 2021, accessed April 28, 20201, https://www.christianitytoday.com/news/2021/april/rene-padilla-died-integral-mission-latin-american-theology.html.

61 Ajith Fernando, "Mission and Evangelism," *ESV.org*, accessed October 13, 2020, https://www.esv.org/resources/esv-global-study-bible/mission-and-evangelism/.

62 Keith Ferdinando, "Mission: A Problem of Definition," *Themelios* 33.1 (2008), 59.

63 *Missio Dei* is a Latin theological term that can be translated as "mission of God." The Church is invited to participate in God's mission in the world. God and God's mission are far beyond the scope and capacity of the Church. Although the Church serves in partnership with God, God's mission is not dependent on the faithfulness or ability of the Church. "The term *missio Dei*, itself has a long history and can be traced at least as far back as Augustine. It was Aquinas who first used the term to describe the activity of the triune God; the father sending the Son and the Son sending the Spirit. In a modern setting; Karl Barth, in a 1932 paper, set out the idea that mission was God's work and that authentic church mission must be in response to God's *missio*." From "Missio Dei and the Mission of the Church," *Wyclffe Global Alliance*, accessed February 1, 2021, https://www.wycliffe.net/more-about-what-we-do/papers-and-articles/missio-dei-and-the-mission-of-the-church/.

64 David J. Bosch, *Transforming Mission: Paradigm Shifts in Theology of Mission* (Maryknoll: Orbis Books, 1991), 519.

65 David Barrett and Todd Johnson, "World Christian Trends across 22 Centuries, AD 30–AD 2200" in *World Christian Trends*, 2001, accessed August 9, 2018, https://archive.gordonconwell.edu/ockenga/research/documents/gd04.pdf.

66 "Global Christianity: A Look at the Status of Christianity in 2018," *Center for the Study of Global Christianity at Gordon-Conwell Theological Seminary*, accessed August 8, 2020, https://archive.gordonconwell.edu/ockenga/research/documents/GlobalChristianityinfographic.pdfPg1.pdf.

67 "Global Statistics: All People Groups," *Joshua Project: a ministry of Frontier Ventures*, accessed August 8, 2020, https://www.joshuaproject.net/people_groups/statistics.

68 "About: Our Impact," *Wycliffe Bible Translators*, accessed October 10, 2020, https://www.wycliffe.org.uk/about/our-impact/.

69 The Hunger Project, "Know Your World: Facts about Hunger and Poverty," accessed August 8, 2020, https://www.thp.org/knowledge-center/know-your-world-facts-about-hunger-poverty/.

70 The Hunger Project, "Know Your World."

71 "Can the Super Rich Help the Regular Rich Solve Their Problem, Asks Empty Tomb, Inc.," *Religion News Service*, April 16, 2019, accessed August 10, 2020, https://religionnews.com/2019/04/16/can-the-super-rich-help-the-regular-rich-solve-their-problem-asks-empty-tomb-inc/.

72 The Hunger Project, "Know Your World."

73 Mark R. Baxter, *The Coming Revolution: Because Status Quo Missions Won't Finish the Job* (Mustang: Tate Publishing, 2007), 12.

74 John Ronsvalle and Sylvia Ronsvalle, *Empty Tomb, inc. Executive Summary, The State of Church Giving through 2017: What a Can-Do Attitude in the Church+$16 Billion Can Do in Jesus' Name for the Children Dying in the Promise Gap* (n. p.: Wipf & Stock, 2019), 73-75.

75 Matthew Branaugh and Chris Lutes (eds), *How Churches Spend Their Money: 2019 Executive Report – An Inside Look at the Church Budget Priorities Study Conducted by Christianity Today's Church Law & Tax* (n.p.: Christianity Today, 2019), 5.

76 The Traveling Team, "Missions Stats: The Current State of the World," accessed August 10, 2020, http://www.thetravelingteam.org/stats.

77 Sylvia Ronsvalle, "Empty Tomb, Inc. Research Explores the Connection Between Declining Giving Patterns and the Lack of a Positive Agenda for Affluence," *Cision: PRWeb*, May 28, 2018, accessed August 9, 2020, https://www.prweb.com/releases/2018/05/prweb15519876.htm.

78 J. Herbert Kane, *Wanted: World Christians* (Grand Rapids: Baker Book, 1986).

79 James Baldwin, "As Much Truth As One Can Bear," *New York Times*, January 14, 1962.

80 David Platt, "Risk It All for Christian Mission," July 6, 2020, accessed December 4, 2020, https://www.youtube.com/watch?v=hOESKzmq4rI.

81 John Kay, "Rolling Stone's 500 Greatest Songs of All Time," *Rolling Stone*, December 11, 2011, accessed November 2, 2019, https://www.rollingstone.com/music/music-lists/500-greatest-songs-of-all-time-151127/steppenwolf-born-to-be-wild-70782/.

82 Steven M. Lukes, "Individualism," *Encyclopedia Britannica*, January 14, 2020, accessed January 3, 2021, https://www.britannica.com/topic/individualism.

83 David Kern, "Surviving the Apocalypse with Help from Charles Taylor," *Think Christian*, June 15, 2016, accessed November 22, 2021, https://thinkchristian.net/surviving-the-apocalypse-with-help-from-charles-taylor.

84 Shane Claiborne, interviewed by Heidi Wilcox, *Thrive with Asbury Seminary*, podcast, accessed July 1, 2021, https://thrive.asburyseminary.edu/mr-shane-claiborne-living-like-jesus-meant-what-he-said/.

85 David F. White and Sarah F. Farmer, eds., *Joy: A Guide for Youth Ministry* (n.p.: Wesley's Foundery, 2020), 6.

86 Walter Besant, quoted by Michael Press, "The Lying Pen of the Scribes: A Nineteenth-Century Dead Sea Scroll," *The Appendix*, September 11, 2014, accessed March 25, 2021, https://theappendix.net/issues/2014/7/the-lying-pen-of-the-scribes-a-nineteenth-century-dead-sea-scroll.

87 Dallas Willard, "Why Bother with Discipleship?," *Renovaré*, October 1995, accessed October 1, 2020, https://renovare.org/articles/why-bother-with-discipleship-1.

88 Soon after Kathy admitted to being a "fat" Christian, she began to exercise her faith by reaching out to international students at the University of Alabama. This ministry of service, hospitality, and witness has continued for over fifteen years.

89 Martin Luther, "An Introduction to St. Paul's Letter to the Romans," quoted by Ron Smith, "Martin Luther's Definition of Faith," *Sola Fidelity*, April 5, 2008, accessed September 7, 2018, https://solafidelity.wordpress.com/2008/04/05/martin-luthers-definition-of-faith/.

90 Josh Womack, "Monday Message No. 29: The Book of Jonah," *Womack Financial*, emailed to author October 21, 2019.

91 Billy Still, *The Jawbone of a Carnivore: Praying the Pathway to Peace* (London: Austin Macauley, 2019), 26–27.

92 William Wilberforce, quoted by Kay Marshall Strom, *Once Blind: The Life of John Newton* (Downers Grove: IVP, 2008), 225.

93 Josh Wilson, vocal performance of "Dream Small," written by Ben Glover and Josh Wilson, released March 2, 2018, on album *Don't Look Back* (EP) by Black River Christian.

94 Laura Messina, email to the author, November 1, 2019.

95 Billy Still, email to the author, November 5, 2019.

96 James C. Collins, *Good to Great: Why Some Companies Make the Leap... and Others Don't* (n.p.: Harper Business, 2001).

97 Scott Moore, "This or That: Patience as a Fruit of the Spirit," sermon at One Hope Church, Tuscaloosa, Alabama, October 10, 2021.

98 Francis Chan, *Crazy Love: Overwhelmed by a Relentless God* (Colorado Springs: David C. Cook, 2013), chap. 5, Kindle.

99 Paul Heinz, "Adding to One's Life Story (part 2)," *Original Fiction, Music & Essays*, January 25, 2017, accessed March 22, 2019, http://www.paulheinz.com/paul-heinz-blog/tag/James+Taylor.

100 Mark Greene, *Thank God It's Monday* (n.p.: KREGE, 2019).

101 Todd Massey, email to the author, December 7, 2020.

102 "Darren Walker: How the Head of the Ford Foundation Wants to Change Philanthropy," interview of Darren Walker by Lesley Stahl, *CBS 60 Minutes*, April 4, 2021, accessed April 4, 2021, https://www.cbsnews.com/news/darren-walker-ford-foundation-60-minutes-2021-04-04/.

103 George H. W. Bush, "President George H. W. Bush's 1989 Speech in Memphis Honoring Volunteers" by Jennifer Pignolet, *Memphis Commercial Appeal*, Dec. 1, 2018, accessed December 2, 2020, https://www.commercialappeal.com/story/news/local/2018/12/01/president-george-h-w-bush-1989-speech-memphis-commercial-appeal-lawn-honoring-volunteers/2175950002/.

104 Pauline Hord, interview by the author on November 17, 2003 in the Hord home. Transcript by Laura Messina.

105 Mamie Till-Mobley and Christopher Benson, *Death of Innocence: The Story of the Hate Crime that Changed America* (New York: Random House, 2003), 251.

106 Steve Corbett and Brian Fikkert, *When Helping Hurts: How to Alleviate Poverty Without Hurting the Poor ... and Yourself* (Chicago: Moody Publishers, 2009); Marvin Olasky, *The Tragedy of American Compassion* (Washington, DC: Regnery Publishing, 1994).

107 Kim Knight, "Enigma Code: Innovation That Saved 14 Million Lives," *The Mobility Forum*, accessed February 13, 2022, https://themobilityforum.net/2020/06/11/enigma-code-innovation-that-saved-14-million-lives/.

108 William MacAskill, *Doing Good Better: How Effective Altruism Can Help You Make a Difference* (New York: Penguin, 2015), introduction, Kindle.

109 Effective Altruism, "Effective Altruism," accessed November 1, 2021, https://www.effectivealtruism.org.

110 A list of other thought leaders includes Abhijit Banerjee and Esther Duflo, founders of the Poverty Action Lab; Ben Todd and William MacAskill, founders of 80,000 Hours; Hilary Greaves and Theron Pummer, editors of *Effective Altruism: Philosophical Issues* (2019); Cari and Dustin Moskovitz, founders of Good Ventures; Alex Foster, CEO of Effective Giving; and Liv Boeree and Igor Kurganov, cofounders of Raising for Effective Giving (REG). A short list of other organizations that work in this area would include Open Philanthropy, Give Well, Charity Watch, and Excellence in Giving. Many universities, including Stanford, London School of Economics, and the University of Miami, include course offerings on effective altruism. In more recent years, people who identify themselves as Christians began to create likeminded organizations: Christian Effective Altruism Project and Effective Altruism for Christians. The author is not affiliated with any of these organizations.

111 My use of the word "effective" relates to the concepts of stewardship, excellence, and impact. Those seeking to be effective will ask questions such as "What path or method will use our available resources to best achieve the goals God has given us?" and "Is the time, energy, finances and prayer we invested getting us closer to the goal?" Ineffectiveness that is ignored is poor stewardship and a dim light at best.

112 Here is a partial list of Bible references that relate to God's strategy, the strategic choices seen in the life of Jesus, and the ways the early Church approached ministry: Genesis 12:1–3; Joshua 6:20; 1 Chronicles 12:32; Psalm 67; 146:7–9; Proverbs 19:2; Isaiah 49:6– 60:3; Matthew 5:14–16; 9:35–38; 10:1–8, 16; 25:1–30; Mark 4:21; 5:19; 7:36; Luke 4:42–43; 5:19; 8:16; 10:1–2, 29–37; 14:28–32; John 1:14; 3:16; 6:12; 7:1–6; Acts 2:14; 3:12; 5:33–35; 11:22–23; 14:26; 19:8–10; 20:20; Romans 5:6, 8; 15:20–21; 1 Corinthians 16: 8–9; 2 Corinthians 10:15–16; Galatians 2:1–2; Ephesians 5:8, 15–17; Colossians 4:3–5, 17; 2 Timothy 2:2; Titus 3:14; 1 Peter 2:9; 1 John 3:17–18.

113 From chapter 5, "God's Mystifying Method": "The vertical line in the cross reminds us of the interaction between holy and loving God and the children of faith. God reaches down to us in grace, and we respond in faith, confession, praise, and allegiance. The horizontal line in the Cross reminds us that joining God in mission to lost and hurting people is vitally connected to authentic faith."

114 Bob Lupton is founder and director of Focused Community Strategies (FCS), a nonprofit organization based in Atlanta that empowers neighborhoods to thrive. Lupton has authored important missions strategy books including *Toxic Charity, Theirs is the Kingdom, Renewing the City,* and *Charity Detox*; John Perkins is founder of the Christian Community Development Association (CCDA). The ministry began in Mississippi but spread to other states. I was particularly impacted by two of Perkins's books, *A Quiet Revolution: The Christian Response to Human Need, a Strategy for Today* (Word Books, 1976), and *Beyond Charity: The Call to Christian Community Development* (Baker Books, 1993).

115 Two helpful books by Ray Bakke: *A Theology as Big as the City* (IVP Academic, 1997) and *The Urban Christian* (IVP Academic, 1987).

116 Esther Duflo, "Social Experiments to Fight Poverty," *TED Talk*, February 2010, accessed January 22, 2022, http://www.ted.com/talks/esther_duflo_ social_experiments_to_fight_poverty.

117 Henry Cloud, *Necessary Endings: The Employees, Businesses, and Relationships that All of Us Have to Give Up in Order to Move Forward* (New York: Harper Collins, 2010), 7.

118 David McCullough, *John Adams* (New York: Simon & Schuster, 2001), chap. 1, Kindle.

119 Contact the author to learn about a process that helps Christians develop a short (3-4 minute), gracious, and clear faith story that is understandable even if the listener has a far different faith background or culture.

120 Timothy Tennent addresses the role of churches around the world in meeting the diverse and overwhelming needs of humankind. "The rise of global immigration, increased diversity, the impact of globalization, and

the increased fragmentation of societies have given rise to a situation where the 'center' and the 'periphery' have merged in new and surprising ways. The church and the mission field are both 'here' and 'there.' Missions can now be advanced as much by a Western agent relocating to North Africa or to an immigrant community in an urban city of the United States, as by a Brazilian missionary moving to China or an African Christian working in London or Los Angeles. Every region of the world has a Christian center, and every region of the world encompasses people groups without the gospel." Timothy Tennent, *Invitation to World Missions: A Trinitarian Missiology for the Twenty-first Century* (Grand Rapids: Kregel, 2010), chap. 16, Kindle.

121 The author is experienced in this type of coaching and is happy to serve congregations and families who desire greater joy and impact in their service and giving.

122 Partners International is a trusted mission partner for churches and families. "Our vision is that local ministries in the least-reached, least resourced nations will be proclaiming the Gospel to every person and building a thriving church for every people." https://www.partnersintl.org/.

123 Copyright information was not found. Some sources suggest that the original words and music were by L. Casebolt and Betty Pulkingham.

124 This list of defining characteristics is a breakdown of the four ways strategic Christians shine as shared at the end of chapter 9.

125 Steve Case, "Steve Case: Get Ready, the Internet is about to Change Again. Here's How," *Washington Post Online: Capital Business*, May 30, 2015, accessed July 19, 2019, https://www.washingtonpost.com/business/capitalbusiness/steve-case-get-ready-the-internet-is-about-to-change-again-heres-how/2015/05/29/d6c87f6c-0493-11e5-bc72-f3e16bf50bb6_story.html.

126 Standards of Excellence in Short-Term Mission (SOE), "Standards of Excellence in Short-Term Mission," accessed December 11, 2021, https://soe.org/about/.

127 *Les Misérables*, a 1998 film adaptation of Victor Hugo's 1862 novel of the same name, directed by Bille August, starring Liam Neeson, Geoffrey Rush et al, directed by Bille August, Sony Pictures; movie script posted by Scripts, accessed March 18, 2018 at https://www.scripts.com/script/les_miserables_12459.

128 William Wilberforce as quoted by Kevin Belmonte, *William Wilberforce: A Hero for Humanity* (Grand Rapids: Zondervan, 2009), chap. 5, Kindle.

129 Clive Calver, quoted by Dennis Whalen, "Less than One Percent," *The Alliance*, September 2007, accessed February 10, 2020, https://legacy.cmalliance.org/alife/less-than-one-percent/.

130 I did not make it to the top of Wulongshan that day. I decided that the risk was not worth the possible benefit. It was a good decision. I did, however, summit two times that summer with friends and family.

131 "Worth," *TheFreeDictionary.com*, accessed May 19, 2021, https://idioms. thefreedictionary.com/worth.

132 The Franklin Institute, "Edison's Lightbulb," accessed May 5, 2021, https:// www.fi.edu/history-resources/edisons-lightbulb.

133 David McCullough, *The Wright Brothers* (New York: Simon & Schuster, 2015), chap. 5, Kindle.

134 David F. White and Sarah F. Farmer, eds., *Joy: A Guide for Youth Ministry* (n.p.: Wesley's Foundery, 2020), 3–4.

135 Brian Hardin, "August 12, 2020," *Daily Audio Bible*, accessed August 12, 2020, https://player.dailyaudiobible.com/dab/08122020.

136 "William Wilberforce, Antislavery Politician," *Christianity Today: Christian History*, August 8, 2008, accessed August 12, 2020, https://www. christianitytoday.com/history/people/activists/william-wilberforce.html.

137 *Christianity Today: Christian History*, "William Wilberforce".

138 Chris Hodges, "The Prayer of Faith," sermon at Church of the Highlands, Birmingham, Alabama, November 8, 2020.

139 Tom Marino, email to author, January 22, 2019.

140 David McCullough, *The Wright Brothers,* chap. 2.

141 David McCullough, *The Wright Brothers*, chap. 2.

142 *Finding Neverland*, directed by Marc Foster, released 2004 by Miramax, starring Johnny Depp, Kate Winslet, Julie Christie, et al.

143 Alan Hirsch, "Why I Do the Things I Do," June 27, 2015, accessed January 22, 2020, https://www.alanhirsch.org/blog/2015/6/27/why-i-do-the-things-i-do.

144 Adam Grant, *Think Again: The Power of Knowing What You Don't Know* (n.p.: Viking, 2021), 4.

145 Edvin H. Robertson, ed., Edvin H. Robertson and John Bowden, trans., *No Rusty Swords: Letters, Lectures and Notes from the Collected Works of Dietrich Bonhoeffer, Vol. 1,* (London: Collins, 1965), 225.

146 John Perkins, *Let Justice Roll Down: John Perkins Tells His Own Story* (Ventura: G/L Regal, 1976).

147 C. S. Lewis, *Mere Christianity* (San Francisco: Harper, 2001), 164.

148 Richard Rohr, *Breathing Under Water: Spirituality and the Twelve Steps* (n.p.: Franciscan Media, 2011), 31.

149 Don Richardson, "A Man for All Seasons," in *Perspectives on the World Christian Movement: A Reader*, Ralph D. Winter and Steven C. Hawthorne, eds (Pasadena: William Carey, 1981), 87.

150 Matthew Smith, "Rumble in the Jungle: What Animals Would Win in a Fight?," *YouGovAmerica*, May 13, 2021, accessed February 2, 2022, https://today.yougov.com/topics/society/articles-reports/2021/05/13/ lions-and-tigers-and-bears-what-animal-would-win-f.

151 "What is Albedo?," *World Atlas*, accessed September 30, 2019, https://www.worldatlas.com/what-is-albedo.html.

152 Fraser Cain, "Moon Albedo," *Universe Today: Space and Astronomy News*, October 23, 2008, accessed October 2, 2019, https://www.universetoday.com/19981/moon-albedo/.

153 Carol Lee Hamrin with Stacey Bieler, *Salt and Light: Lives of Faith that Shaped Modern China* (Eugene: Pickwick Publications, 2009), 3, 12.

154 Norman H. Cliff, *Fierce the Conflict: The Moving Stories of How Eight Chinese Christians Suffered for Jesus Christ and Remained Faithful* (Ontario: Joshua Press, 2001), 33.

155 Cornelius Tacitus, *The Annals*, 15.44, as provided on Perseus Digital Library, Alfred John Church and William Jackson Brodribb, eds., accessed April 2, 2020, http://www.perseus.tufts.edu/hopper/text?doc=Perseus:text:1999.02.0078:book=15:chapter=44.

156 Robert Lee Long, "A Message of Faith and the Power of Prayer," *Desoto Times-Tribune*, October 31, 2013, accessed February 11, 2021, http://www.desototimes.com/news/a-message-of-faith-and-the-power-of-prayer/article_0379acf2-f0b9-5723-8d77-0e6699484a2d.html.

157 Not every faithful and strategic Christian will make choices like the Lipscombs. People grieve and adjust to loss in a variety of ways and on various timelines. But every child of God has the opportunity to use their pain for God's glory and for the good of the world. Your witness may not involve the media, you may impact only one person, and you may need more time to be ready to shine. But God will help you find the right time and opportunity to shine as a special kind of light, a light that knows the hopelessness of darkness. God can use your real pain as a platform to provide light and love to someone in darkness. This is part of the meaning of Romans 8:28.

158 Timothy Tennent, *Invitation to World Missions: A Trinitarian Missiology for the Twenty-first Century* (Grand Rapids: Kregel, 2010), conclusion, Kindle.

159 The Cash Family, "Last Night's Community Meeting ... what a gift," *CashCrewshipBlogspot,* January 24, 2014, accessed July 1, 2020, https://cashcrewship.blogspot.com/2014/01. For more, check out Wess Stafford's excellent book regarding the strategic importance of loving and ministering to children, *Too Small to Ignore: Why Children Are the Next Big Thing,* 2005.

160 Pauline Hord, interview by the author on November 17, 2003 in the Hord home. Transcript by Laura Messina.

161 William P. Young, *The Shack: Where Tragedy Confronts Eternity* (n.p.: Windblown Media, 2007), chap. 15, Kindle.

162 Written by Andrew Peterson and Ben Shive, recording by Shane and Shane, "Is He Worthy (Live)" from the album *Hymns Live,* released 2019 by Well House Records.

Printed in the United States
by Baker & Taylor Publisher Services